£13.07

D1428744

An Essential Guide To
AMERICAN
POLITICS
And The
AMERICAN
POLITICAL
SYSTEM

Kenneth L. Hill

authorHOUSE®

AuthorHouse™
1663 Liberty Drive
Bloomington, IN 47403
www.authorhouse.com
Phone: 1-800-839-8640

Published by AuthorHouse   07/19/2012

ISBN: 978-1-4772-4916-1 (sc)
ISBN: 978-1-4772-4915-4 (hc)
ISBN: 978-1-4772-4914-7 (e)

Library of Congress Control Number: 2012913135

The format of this book is rather simple. It starts with the Revolutionary War and then follows events leading to the 1789 Constitutional Convention. After analyzing events at the convention, the book then offers an analysis of the three branches of government. Then we analyze some of the important components of the American political system such as political parties and presidential primaries. The last section of the book deals with political terms in alphabetical order. There is some duplication but it is intentional. For example, the Connecticut Compromise is in the section dealing with the Constitutional Convention but readers will also find it in the alphabetical section.

CONTENTS

DECLARATION OF INDEPENDENCE

The Declaration of Independence, approved by the continental Congress in 1776, declared the thirteen colonies to be free and independent of Great Britain's rule. The ideas in the document, authored by Thomas Jefferson, justified the revolution against unjust rule and has served as justification for revolutions in many places around the world ever since. The Declaration had several purposes. It explained why the colonists could not continue under British rule. Its message is that all governments are subject to restraints to prevent abuse of authority. Individuals have certain inalienable rights governments cannot take away and should not abuse. This claim remains valid today but some governments reject restrictions on their power. They behave as though there are no legitimate restraints. Jefferson's ideas are incompatible with non-democratic political systems that restrict or abuse fundamental freedoms. The Declaration was also a repudiation of certain laws put into place by George III including the Intolerable Acts, the Stamp Act, the Tea Tax, the Quartering Act, and others. The Declaration influenced the French rebels determined to curb the absolute power of the French government under the leadership of Louis XVI. When the French rebelled they often relied on many of the same slogans that inspired Americans to rebel against George

III. A major purpose of the Declaration was to unify the colonists behind the cause of independence and to win foreign support as well. Foreign governments were unlikely to support a reform movement that simply wanted some changes in the way Great Britain ruled its colonies. The Declaration has lost none of its validity or relevance with the passing of time. It influenced President Wilson's Fourteen Points and President Roosevelt's speech in 1941 embracing the Four Freedoms. The Declaration influenced provisions of many international documents including the 1945 United Nations Charter and the Universal Declaration of Human Rights approved by the United Nations in 1948. Many nationalist leaders in the Afro-Asian world relied on the Declaration after World War II to justify their fight for independence and an end to colonial rule. The independence of many colonies after the war was one of the major events of the twentieth century. The Declaration of Independence and the Constitution have distinct purposes. The Declaration justified the revolution. The Constitution deals with process, structure and the organization of the American political system.

TREATY OF PARIS

In 1783, American and British officials signed the Treaty of Paris ending the Revolutionary War. A year later Congress ratified the treaty negotiated by Benjamin Franklin, John Jay, and James Madison. Great Britain recognized the independence of the thirteen states. The treaty consisted of ten articles dealing with items such as territorial boundaries, fishing rights, the payment of debts, property rights, the confiscation of property, prisoners of war, captured territory, and access to the Mississippi River. After completing the treaty, many disputes developed between the two countries because of conflicting interpretations regarding certain treaty provisions. Both sides were guilty of numerous violations. Individual states violated treaty provisions and there was little the national government could do to remedy the situation. Many Americans refused to pay debts owed to the British and many refused to return confiscated properties. The British government violated treaty provisions without fear of retaliation. The British refused to return captured slaves and failed to vacate some captured territories. Relations between Great Britain and the United States remained strained for many years after the war. The two countries resolved some of their conflicting interpretations of the Treaty of Paris when they signed the Jay Treaty in 1794. Despite the resolution of many of their differences, the two countries again went to war in 1812. Despite winning independence, there was no guarantee the union of thirteen states would endure and prosper. The new nation had to cope with many complex problems, both foreign and domestic. The leaders of the new nation soon realized that finding solutions to these problems would take time. In many ways the two sets of problems, foreign and domestic, were connected and this made the search for solutions more difficult. U.S. ties to Great Britain were complicated by the fact that many Americans were ambivalent about relations with Great Britain after the Revolutionary War. Some Americans favored a closer relationship but others were more comfortable with closer ties to France. George Washington supported a policy of neutrality. He did not want the United States too closely aligned to the policies of any European state. The Treaty of Paris left the United States the ruler of all the territory east of the Mississippi. George Washington envisioned the United States a great power without rivals other than some Indian tribes.

CONTINENTAL CONGRESS 1774-1789

The Continental Congress convened in 1774. It was a unicameral body meaning it was composed of only one house. All the states except

Georgia sent representatives to the Congress that had a membership of fifty six members, each selected by their state legislature. Members of the Congress had to decide how to respond to the actions taken by the British government in response to Boston Tea Party. The Continental Congress ruled the country during a time of uncertainty and had to cope with many complex problems without having adequate power to do so effectively. It did institute a boycott of British goods and this contributed to the decision on the part of the British to deal more harshly with the colonies. Initially, delegates to the Congress did not intend to seek independence from Great Britain but they did demand changes in the way the British government dealt with the colonies. King George III did not think it was necessary to appease the colonists and this convinced many members of the Continental Congress that independence was their only option. In 1775, King George III formally accused the colonies of rebellion. That same year, the Second Continental Congress convened and was responsible for conducting the war for independence that had already begun. Military clashes between the two sides spread throughout the colonies. In 1776, the Second Continental Congress approved the Declaration of Independence. There was much support for such a declaration because delegates to the Congress did not think they could win any international support without it. Foreign governments would have no incentive for supporting a rebellion if the only goal of the colonists was to win political and economic reforms. The leaders of the revolution had to determine how to govern the new country. They completed that task in 1777, when the Continental Congress approved the Articles of Confederation that established a new political framework to govern the United States. The states approved the Articles in 1781. The Congress dissolved in 1789 when the states ratified the new Constitution.

ARTICLES OF CONFEDERATION

In 1777, the Continental Congress approved the Articles of Confederation consisting of thirteen articles. They became operative in 1781 after all thirteen states gave their approval. They remained in force until 1789. The Articles spelled out how the new government would function and reflected the fact the colonists had just rebelled against the authority of King George III. The thirteen states needed a legitimate government to conduct relations with other governments around the world but the authors made certain the national government did not have more power than they thought was necessary. The Articles served as a constitution for the nation as a whole but individual states were also writing constitutions for the conduct of their own affairs. This was unusual because at that time, most countries, including Great Britain, did not have a written constitution. The authors of the Articles shared the fear most Americans had of executive power at the national level and therefore made no provision for an executive such as a president, a king, or a prime minister. Not only did the Articles limit the power of the national government, they also conferred sovereignty on each of the thirteen states. They were for all practical purposes independent of each other. **All** thirteen states had to approve the Articles before they became operative. They all gave their approved and welcomed the fact that the national government was granted few powers. A weak national government was unlikely to abuse its powers because the Articles granted so few powers to the national government. In many respects, the states viewed each other as rivals. During the colonial period, many of the colonies had closer relations with Great Britain than they had with each other. They relied on the **British government for their well-being and protection. They were a part of the British colonial empire with all the advantages that entailed. Being part of a great empire had many advantages but most of these were lost when the colonies became independent.**

ARTICLES OF CONFEDERATION:
THE NATIONAL GOVERNMENT

Under the Articles of Confederation, the national government had no executive office such as a president or a prime minister. The national government could deal with state governments but could not deal directly with people within the states. This inability to deal directly with its citizens is what differentiates a confederation from a federal or a unitary government. The victorious colonies, mindful of the abuses of George III, intended to limit the power of the national government. The Articles effectively accomplished that objective. When the national government wanted to raise funds, it did so by asking states to provide the money. The states would then decide whether to comply or ignore the request. The national government could not directly tax the citizens and therefore had to rely on the state governments. The same was true for military service and many other tasks the national government needed to perform. The national government would ask each state to provide X number of people for military service but states need not comply. The refusal of some states to meet their obligations encouraged others to do the same. Most states failed to honor some of their obligations and there was no penalty for doing so. The national government did have certain powers that theoretically did not require the approval of states but often did require their cooperation and this enabled the states to compromise the powers of the national government. These powers included such things as the power to coin money, negotiate treaties, and exchange diplomatic personnel, including ambassadors. Problems arose, however, when some states issued their own currencies and interpreted treaties as they saw fit. States frequently bypassed the national government and negotiated directly with foreign governments. What was significant about the Articles was not the power granted to the national government but the powers denied. The central government could print money but it had little if any value because there was nothing to back up the value of the currency. This weakness had a major impact on trade with other countries and trade between the states. Some states issued their own currency. The currencies they issued had the same problem as did the national currency—there was nothing to back up its value. After the Revolutionary War, the debt burden of the national government was a major problem because it did not have adequate funds to repay its debts. Many of the Founding Fathers believed paying the debt was a national priority for reasons of prestige, honor, and economic necessity. Treaties negotiated by the national government were also a problem because ratification needed the approval of all thirteen states. Foreign governments did not want to negotiate treaties with the United States because of the approval process and the inability of the national government to guarantee adherence to treaty provisions, once approved. Foreign governments were more interested in exploiting the weakness of the United States rather than cooperating with it. Some states also had their own foreign policy thus making it difficult for the national government to deal with foreign powers. The national government simply did not have the power or authority to do what people ordinarily expect the government to do including such things as raising an army, paying debts, and maintaining order. Amending the Articles to give the national government more power was difficult because all thirteen states had to agree to any amendments. Getting all the states to approve provisions to strengthen the authority of the national government was a daunting task. States were reluctant to yield any power to a higher authority.

ARTICLES OF CONFEDERATION: STATE POWERS

After winning independence, the United States was composed of thirteen states. Each state had one vote in the national legislature regardless of its geographical size or population. The states retained all powers not expressly granted to the national government. The Articles permitted each state to be sovereign, free, and independent but unlike sovereign nations, states could not send or receive ambassadors from foreign countries. The Articles did not grant the national government many powers. The vote of nine states was necessary to pass legislation but amending the Articles required a unanimous vote, as did ratification of treaties. During the period of the Articles, the need for unanimity nullified the amendatory process thus making it difficult to correct weaknesses at the national level to better govern the country. Each of the thirteen states controlled most of its own affairs but that left each of them weak and vulnerable to foreign powers. Individual states confronted many problems similar to those the national government had to confront. The states had huge debts and were unable to pay their bills or meet expenses. Most had severe economic problems generating considerable discontent because state governments could do little to ease poverty or promote prosperity. The result of government weakness at both the national and state levels threatened the well-being and future of the new nation. The revolt against British authority was successful but this did not mean the newly created nation could do what its subjects expected. There was a growing recognition that the national government needed additional powers to cope with its many problems. The question was how to grant the national government more power without threatening the sovereignty of the states. This was the dilemma. After the American Revolution and the adoption of the Articles, states jealously guarded their sovereignty. They fought the revolution to limit the power of government and were determined to limit the power of the new government established after the revolution. The authors of the Articles delegated to the national government relatively few powers and those often needed the cooperation of states for their implementation. The conflict between those individuals supporting or opposing a stronger national government continued throughout the period of the Articles of Confederation, 1781-1789. The conflict continued throughout the Constitutional Convention and the debates for and against ratification of the Constitution. Disagreement about how much power the national government should have has remained a characteristic of American politics right up until the present time. The rise of the Tea Party after the 2010 congressional elections renewed the debate. A primary purpose of the Tea Party was to limit the power of the national government.

ARTICLES OF CONFEDERATION: ECONOMIC ISSUES

During the period of the Articles of Confederation, 1781-1789, the country faced numerous economic problems the national government was unable to cope with because of inadequate powers. Some of the problems confronting the government after winning independence included the inability to raise money, difficulty paying debts, inability to tax people directly, and a weak military inadequate to protect the nation's national interests. The country no longer enjoyed the advantages of being a British colony. The national government had insufficient power to deal with conflicts between the states or conflicts between the states and the national government. There were navigational disputes between and among the states that hampered interstate commerce. The national government did not control interstate commerce and this failure allowed states to discriminate against each other and they often did. They did so to benefit people within the state regardless of the adverse effects such policies had on other states. Individual states had to pay high tariffs to have their goods enter foreign markets. States did not have much bargaining power when dealing with foreign governments because each state negotiated for its own benefit. Foreign governments often practiced a policy of divide and rule. The United States lacked a strong stable currency and this also hampered trade with other countries. Not only did the national government have major economic problems, the states did also for many of the same reasons. The expectation that freedom would bring economic prosperity proved false. Economic problems were so severe as to threaten the very existence of the confederation. Winning the revolution did not bring the benefits many thought it would.

ARTICLES OF CONFEDERATION: FOREIGN POLICY ISSUES

The national government, during the period of the Articles, had to deal with many foreign policy problems but did not have the power to do so effectively. The United States had problems with Canada, Great Britain, France, Spain, and Indian tribes. Problems included territorial boundaries, treaty violations, use of the Mississippi River, and international commerce and finance. Before transferring control to France, Spain controlled the New Orleans port and this enabled it to disrupt interstate trade and trade between the states and foreign countries. The United States and Spain also had disputes over territorial boundaries in Florida. At the time, Spain was a major international power. Great Britain refused to negotiate a commercial trade agreement with the United States and encouraged Indian uprisings that were often violent. Despite the end of the revolution in 1783, the British refused to vacate military forts as required to do so by the Treaty of Paris. The United States had territorial disputes with Canada that often erupted into violence. Individual states frequently conducted their foreign affairs without consulting the national government. In some respects the United States had fourteen different foreign policies—one for each state and one for the national government. It could not always carry out agreements it entered into thus discouraging foreign governments from negotiating agreements. Some agreements required the cooperation of the states that was not forthcoming if there was no tangible benefit for doing so.

SHAYS REBELLION 1786

Shays rebellion began in Massachusetts in 1786 but the rebellion had supporters in other states because of similar conditions. There were several causes for the rebellion including the policy of banks seizing property of individuals failing to pay their debts. Some of these individuals, including Daniel Shays, were patriotic Americans and veterans of the Revolutionary War. At the time of the rebellion, courts could sentence people to spend time in a debtor's prison. This aggravated the economic plight of the farmers and fanned their sense of betrayal. They did not support and participate in the revolution expecting this kind of treatment from their fellow Americans. The debtors believed their only recourse was to rebel against the system imposing the high taxes and taking their land when taxes were not paid. The rebels supported printing money to pay their debts but this devalued the currency and worried individuals and institutions that loaned the money. The protection of private property is an essential part of the foundation of democratic government. One of the high points of the rebellion was the raid on a federal arsenal in Massachusetts and the seizure of weapons to use against opponents. The national and state governments did not have the wherewithal to cope with the deteriorating economic conditions or the resulting violence. Shays rebellion ended in 1787 when the governor of Massachusetts raised enough money from private sources to put together a militia. The fact that he had to rely on private sources to deal with the rebellion indicates the nature and severity of the problem. Many national leaders supporting the national government feared that events such as Shays rebellion could cause a civil war with unforeseen consequences. The rebellion strengthened the determination of those individuals wanting to convene a convention to forge a stronger union by delegating more powers to the national government. They thought this required scraping the Articles of Confederation and writing a new governing document. The primary function of every government in the world is the maintenance of order. Shays rebellion demonstrated the need for a stronger government to carry out this primary function. The fact that the governor had to raise money from private sources worried political leaders. It was not a good precedent.

ANNAPOLIS CONVENTION 1786

The Annapolis Convention took place in Annapolis, Maryland in 1786 one month after the start of Shays rebellion. Only twelve delegates from five states attended the meeting including Alexander Hamilton and James Madison. Shays rebellion caused both men deep concern about the nation's future. The primary purpose of the meeting was to find solutions to the many defects in the Articles of Confederation. They were inadequate for dealing with the many problems plaguing the thirteen states including such things as rebellion, poor economic conditions, and rivalries between and among the states. Delegates attending the convention realized they needed more representatives from more states to participate if there was to be any realistic expectation of reform. The delegates wanted any proposed reforms to have wide support to ensure their legitimacy. A limited number of delegates from only five states would not have the authority to do what was necessary. Delegates at Annapolis called for a meeting of all the states to help remedy the defects in the Articles of Confederation. That meeting, the Constitutional Convention, convened in Philadelphia in 1787. By the terms of the Annapolis agreement, the purpose of the convention was to reform the Articles, not to write a new constitution. Those individuals supporting a new constitutional arrangement realized the issues at the proposed convention would be contentious particularly those dealing with the distribution of power between the national and state governments. Many leaders feared the nation would fracture without a new governing order to replace the

Articles of Confederation. The question was not the need to reform but rather what kinds of reforms would be effective and acceptable to all the factions. Different states had different problems and different needs. Reforms required developing a consensus acceptable to all the states. This was a difficult requirement because states often viewed each other as competitors. Individuals were primarily loyal to their states rather than some larger entity such as a nation but states were often lacking in necessary resources to resolve their problems. The problems required a national response.

NEED FOR STRONG NATIONAL GOVERNMENT

Although some prominent Americans opposed convening a convention to remedy defects in the Articles of Confederation, others recognized that delay in making reforms could jeopardize the country's independence. The United States existed in a hostile environment with many adversaries, numerous territorial disputes, deteriorating economic conditions, and an inadequate military to protect America's national security interests. In addition to foreign policy issues, leaders feared the new nation would fail economically if the national government remained weak and unable to control such things as foreign and interstate commerce. There was a growing consensus on the part of America's ruling elite that the Articles were inadequate. More political leaders came to believe that amending the Articles would not be sufficient. In any case, amending the Articles was unlikely because all thirteen states had to give their approval thus making it unlikely the states would approve any amendment. Despite this shared outlook on the need for reforms, there was not much consensus about specific reforms. There was, however, a growing recognition on the need for radical changes. A consensus on specific reforms took time to develop in part because there were many proposals by leaders with strong opinions. Building consensus often required yielding on some points to win support for others. Those advocating reforms had to decide if they should try to salvage the Articles or discard them in favor of a new governing document. Increasingly, many members of the ruling elite at both the national and state levels believed radical change was necessary and therefore the need for a new governing document to strengthen the national government. Those in favor of drafting a new document had difficulty agreeing on the specifics. Other reformers insisted that amendments to the Articles could bring about needed changes. The major issue was whether the country could survive and prosper or would disintegrate. Many delegates thought the individual states could survive with their independence intact only if they supported substantive changes in the distribution of power between the states and the national government. Some critics had difficulty reconciling the idea that creating a strong national government would benefit the states. The two ideas seemed to be contradictory. The delegates at Annapolis did agree to convene another meeting for the purpose of amending the Articles of Confederation.

CONVENING THE CONSTITUTIONAL CONVENTION

The Constitutional Convention convened in Philadelphia in 1787 and was in session from May to September. Delegates elected George Washington as the presiding officer. Selecting Washington was not controversial. At the time, he was the best known most popular American and he enjoyed great respect among the delegates. His willingness to attend the convention guaranteed that other prominent officials would also attend. Fifty-five delegates attended the convention but several prominent Americans did not, including Thomas Jefferson, John Jay, John Adams, Samuel Adams, and John Hancock. Some who did not attend were unable to do so but supported efforts to strengthen the national government. John Adams was serving as Minister to Great

Britain. Jefferson was serving as Minister to France. Patrick Henry refused to attend because he feared what the delegates might do. Samuel Adams also refused to attend for the same reason. John Hancock was ill and unable attend. Rhode Island sent no delegates. Some political leaders at the convention insisted that reforms at the state level would solve the country's problems. Many of them continued to fear granting too much power to the national government. Somewhat uncertain was the meaning of "too much power." Some delegates realized the necessity of granting more power to the national government but wanted to make certain the powers would be limited and not abused. One way to achieve this goal was to retain the confederal form of government. Delegates supporting a stronger national government believed they could discard the confederation and create a federal form of government with sufficient checks to prevent the abuse of power. Delegates wanting to retain the confederation did not agree. They opposed giving the national government too much power and pointed out that delegates came to Philadelphia to revise the Articles, not to discard them. Gradually, more delegates began to accept the need to discard the flawed Articles and start anew. Eventually, some delegates opposed ratifying the Constitution because the delegates exceeded their authority by writing a constitution rather than complying with the amendatory process. James Madison kept notes of the proceedings and they tell us much of what we know about the debates and the many compromises necessary to forge needed agreements. The notes are important because delegates agreed to conduct the sessions in secret. Secrecy required that all the windows of Convention Hall remain closed. During the summer months, Convention Hall was unpleasantly hot. The formal dress of the delegates added to their discomfort. They were eager to complete their work and return home. Rarely, if ever, in American history has such a distinguished group of leaders met to resolve major problems during a time of crisis. Many of the outstanding intellects at the time devoted themselves to the affairs of government. Delegates to the convention were well aware they were engaged in a historically significant project. The opportunity to create a new nation and its political institutions does not often occur. One important fact is that those opposed to any change in the confederation refused to attend the convention. The conflict at the convention was between those seeking to change the articles and those wholly opposed to the articles.

CONSTITUTIONAL CONVENTION: SOME MAJOR ISSUES

The Constitutional Convention convened in 1787. The delegates had to deal with many complex issues needing resolution. The issues included slavery, representation, the distribution of powers between national and state governments, powers of the executive, type of executive, separation of powers, length of term in office, guaranteeing the rights of citizens, and many others. The list of problems needing resolution was daunting. Conflicting opinions about how these problems should be resolved necessitated making many compromise decisions. Any of these issues could have led to deadlock and failure. Some delegates feared that failure to agree to a new constitution might result in a breakup of the confederation. If that occurred, there was no guarantee the individual states could survive. The European powers had several means they could employ, including economic and military powers, to win control of some of the states. Many delegates eventually agreed that the major problems confronting the states required a national response. At the time of the Constitutional Convention, state constitutions contained some basic principles the delegates thought should be included in a national constitution. Some delegates at the convention had a good deal of experience trying to reconcile effective government and political rights. This is basically what the Constitutional Convention was about although initially there was no general agreement on how the reconciliation could work. Delegates were not always confident about what would work politically but they had a good deal of experience with what did not work. Shortly after the convention convened, Governor Edmund Randolph presented the Virginia Plan that called for radical reforms. His plan helped shape the debates at the convention and it soon became evident that his plan, much of which James Madison developed, was not compatible with a confederal form of government. Many delegates with strong political views were committed to making the convention a success even if that required abandoning political preferences to reach a consensus. They came to the convention knowing that major changes were necessary if the union was to survive. The remarkable thing about the convention is the fact that it did succeed. The delegates wrote a constitution, the states ratified it, and it has endured.

CONSTITUTIONAL CONVENTION: VIRGINA PLAN

James Madison authored the Virginia Plan. It called for a two house national legislature. Voters would determine the composition of the lower house. Members of the lower house would then elect members of a second chamber based on nominations submitted by the states. Large states supported the Virginia Plan, small states opposed it. Under the Articles of Confederation all states were equal and they all had one vote in the national legislature regardless of population or geographical size. The Virginia Plan called for the creation of three branches of government and a system of checks and balances. The Virginia Plan was important because it framed the debate about the political structure needed to govern the country. The Virginia Plan was obviously incompatible with a confederal form of government. When Madison's plan became the focus of debate, many delegates quickly realized that his plan, or some version of it, meant scrapping the Articles of Confederation. Getting the delegates to discuss the Virginia Plan demonstrates the importance of controlling the agenda. Making the Virginia Plan the centerpiece of debate forced the delegates to accept, reject, or propose modifications of the plan. The New Jersey delegation rejected the plan thus encouraging the Connecticut delegation to propose a compromise agreement.

CONTITUTIONAL CONVENTION: NEW JERSEY PLAN

Delegates at the Constitutional Convention had to deal with the contentious issue of representation. They had strong opinions about the issue because it would help determine the ability of states to influence legislation at the national level. The New Jersey Plan was one of several plans designed to deal with the representation issue. Proponents of this plan wanted to protect the power and influence of the small states. They supported retaining the confederation but with some minor modifications. The New Jersey Plan proposed creating a unicameral legislature with each state having equal representation regardless of population or geographical size. This was similar to the legislature under the Articles of Confederation. The New Jersey plan did endow the legislative branch with more powers than it had under the Articles. For example, the legislature would be empowered to lay and collect taxes without relying on the states for their cooperation. The more populous states thought the New Jersey plan was unfair because they did not think small and large states should have equal power in the proposed legislature. Fairness became an important issue at the convention. The Connecticut Compromise relied on the New Jersey Plan in determining the structure and role of the Senate but not the House of Representatives. The convention rejected the New Jersey Plan and adopted the Connecticut Plan also known as the Great Compromise.

CONSTITUTIONAL CONVENTION: CONNECTICUT PLAN

Differences between the large and small states regarding representation in the proposed national legislature threatened the hoped for success at the Constitutional Convention. The Virginia Plan for representation would have enabled the largest states to control the legislative process. The New Jersey Plan favored the smaller states. The conflict between those supporting the New Jersey Plan and those supporting the Virginia Plan led to the Connecticut Plan, also called the Great Compromise. The conflict between the large and small states was not just about geographical areas or population. The fact is that the large and small states differed on many issues because they had conflicting interests and different economic priorities. The most important issue, however, was one of fairness. How to reconcile fairness in terms of representation and conflicting economic interests was a difficult problem. Fairness can have many definitions. The Connecticut Compromise combined portions of each, the New Jersey and Virginia plans, thus resolving a major issue. The Great Compromise created a bicameral legislature. Population would determine representation in the House of Representatives but each state would have equal representation in the Senate. The slave states wanted one chamber to represent their states as a means to protect slavery. If a congress consisted of only one house based on population, the plan could endanger the slave states if a sharp increase in the population of the non-slave states occurred. Some delegates at the convention wanted to end slavery immediately or as soon as possible. The southern states wanted to protect their economic interests in part because the economy and the southern lifestyle were connected. The Connecticut Compromise satisfied the representatives of the southern states because the structure of the Senate enabled them to protect southern interests such as slavery. Reconciling the interests of the large and small states was a major accomplishment at the Constitutional

Convention. The Connecticut Compromise helped make certain the approval of the new Constitution.

SLAVERY: THREE-FIFTHS COMPROMISE

The issue of slavery and the slave trade was one of the most contentious issues at the Constitutional Convention. By the time the convention convened, many countries had abolished slavery and the slave trade. Although a considerable number of delegates questioned the morality and legitimacy of slavery, the southern states were committed to the slave system. They also insisted that slaves be included in any numerical count dealing with representation in the proposed legislature. Slaves made up approximately forty percent of the population of the South. If southern states could not count slaves for purposes of representation, they would have less ability in the proposed congress to influence legislation dealing with this issue. For many southerners, slavery was an essential aspect of their economy. Slave owners and those involved in the slave trade were well aware that some delegates at the convention wanted to abolish slavery. It was a divisive issue, politically and morally. Many southerners did not think their states could survive economically without it. In addition to slave labor, southerners considered slaves an investment that could yield an acceptable profit and thereby contribute to an individual's wealth. The buying and selling of slaves could be financially rewarding. There was also the fact that slavery was an integral part of the southern way of life. The delegates at the Constitutional Convention decided to permit the continuation of the slave trade until 1808 and then end it. Regarding representation in the proposed congress, delegates agreed to continue the practice that existed under the Articles of Confederation. Under the Articles, the states counted slaves as three-fifths of a person for tax purposes. Delegates at the convention accepted the three-fifths formula for purposes of representation. The compromise was a major achievement at the convention for without it there would not have been enough delegate support to approve a new constitutional order. The slavery issue and its consequences remained a major problem in American politics long after the Constitutional Convention. For some delegates, having a democratic form of government along with a system of slavery was troubling.

FEDERALISTS PAPERS

Alexander Hamilton, James Madison, and John Jay wrote the Federalist Papers consisting of eighty-five letters and essays to support ratifying the Constitution. They wrote the letters and essays because there was much opposition to ratifying the Constitution led by the Anti-Federalists. The Federalist Papers are remarkable in their defense, analysis, and justification of the Constitution. They also explained and analyzed its underlying principles. The papers remain one of the best sources for understanding the theoretical framework of the American political system although they did not play a significant role in the ratification process outside of New York State. New York ratified the proposed constitution after Virginia and Massachusetts gave their approval. New York's approval was essential if the ratification process was to succeed. The Constitution was controversial and, when the ratification process began, there was no assurance a sufficient number of states would give their approval. The Anti-Federalists led by individuals such as Patrick Henry and George Mason feared the Constitution gave too much power to the national government and therefore endangered the freedom of the American people. The agreement to add a Bill of Rights to the Constitution helped overcome some opposition but many opponents were not appeased.

FEDERALISTS AND ANTI-FEDERALISTS

The two major groups at the Constitutional Convention were the Federalists and the Anti-Federalists. The Anti-Federalists genuinely believed that a strong national government threatened individual freedoms. The Federalists thought the country would fail and disintegrate if the national government did not have sufficient power to cope with its many problems. The government under the Articles of Confederation had insufficient powers to cope with the many challenges confronting the confederation after winning independence. There were prominent individuals in both camps. Patrick Henry, Thomas Paine, and George Mason were leaders of the Anti-Federalist faction. Patrick Henry opposed the Constitution because he thought it violated the Declaration of Independence. James Madison, John Jay, and Alexander Hamilton led the Federalists. These two groups were deeply involved in the ratification process. Ratification of the Constitution was not a certainty. This became evident during the heated debates about the power distribution between the states and the central government and the distribution of power at the national level among the three branches of government. Some delegates wanted a strong executive but others wanted to limit the power of the executive to prevent possible abuses. Abusing governmental powers was a major cause for rebelling against British rule. George III ruled in an arbitrary fashion and failed to recognize the rights of the colonists. He assumed they were his subjects and he alone would determine their rights and freedoms. Many anti-Federalists agreed with Lord Acton that "absolute power corrupts absolutely." The ratification debates were vigorous in most states. The newly written Constitution had many supporters and opponents. Some critics were apprehensive about the Constitution because there was no certainty about how the government would implement its provisions. Some provisions were general in nature to enable the government to meet unanticipated problems. Ratification required the approval of nine states before becoming operative. The Federalists and the Anti-Federalists campaigned in all the states. In June 1787, the New Hampshire state convention approved the Constitution, the ninth state to do so. New York and Virginia were not among the first nine. Without their approval the Constitution would have been of no value. They were too large and too important not to be included in the newly formed union. Shortly after the New Hampshire vote, both states approved the Constitution by a slim margin. Subsequently, North Carolina voted approval. The delegates completed the Constitution in 1787. The states ratified it in 1789. In 1790, Rhode Island was the last of the thirteen states to ratify the Constitution. Despite the fact the Anti-Federalists strongly opposed the Constitution, many of them accepted, however reluctantly, the final vote.

BILL OF RIGHTS

The Bill of Rights, the first ten amendments to the Constitution, was not a part of the original Constitution. Some states threatened to reject the Constitution because of its absence. One fear that emerged during the ratification debates was the prospect of the national government abusing its powers. Colonists rebelled against British rule under George III rule because he threatened basic freedoms. Proponents of a Bill of Rights not only feared the specific grant of power to the national government in the proposed constitution but also the implied powers. The government could define its powers expansively by relying on those clauses in the Constitution such as the "necessary and proper" clause in Article I, section 8, the meaning of which changed significantly with the passing of time. The Anti-Federalists could not predict how judges and government officials would interpret the various articles of the Constitution but they were correct in being apprehensive about what the future might hold. At the time of the Constitutional Convention, most states had a bill of rights to protect people at the state level. Critics believed it was more imperative to have the same protection at the national level. Some delegates such as Alexander Hamilton opposed including a Bill of Rights in the proposed constitution because they feared any rights not included might be excluded, ignored, or denied. Hamilton was not alone in his opposition but to ensure ratification, he changed his position and agreed to add a Bill of Rights. He and other supporters of the Constitution wanted to avoid convening another convention to amend the Constitution for fear a second convention would undo the many compromises already achieved. The Continental Congress approved the Bill of Rights in 1789. The states completed the ratification process in 1791. When the Bill of Rights first passed, it limited the powers of the national government and was not applicable to the states. This limitation was eventually changed. After the Civil War, the government began the process of applying provisions of the Bill of Rights to the states. It is rather ironic that with the passing of time, the Bill of Rights came to restrict the powers of the states and increased the power of the national government.

CONSTITUTIONAL PRINCIPLES: REPRESENTATIVE DEMOCRACY

In a representative democracy people elect members of the government to represent their interests. They also have the power, through the electoral process, to hold elected officials accountable for their actions. This differs from a direct democracy that allows people to govern themselves. It also differs from autocratic systems that deny people participation in the decision-making process. In 1789, when the states ratified the Constitution, people did not have the power to elect the president or members of the Senate. Delegates at the Constitutional Convention were fearful of a government with too much power. Although delegates supported a democratic form of government they also feared mob rule. This is evident by the fact that delegates wanted to limit the ability of the majority to influence government policies. In 1789, only a small percentage of the population was eligible to vote. Women did not have a right to vote and there were voting qualifications that prevented many males from voting. Those eligible to vote could do so only for members of the House of Representatives. State legislatures elected U. S. Senators and this practice remained in force until 1913. From then on voters in the states elected their senators. The Electoral College, not the popular vote, determines who will be president. Critics would like to abolish or reform the Electoral College to make it more representative of the popular vote. Eventually, the government removed or lowered barriers to voting. The government has become more representative with the passing of time. Eligibility to vote now usually requires that potential voters need meet only age and residency requirements and be U.S. citizens. With the passing of time, the government became more representative than it was in 1789. Voting laws and legal decisions extended the franchise, law makers approved legislation protecting basic rights, and the Supreme Court handed down a number of rulings to better protect basic rights.

CONSTITUTIONAL PRINCIPLES: RULE OF LAW

In a political system characterized by the rule of law, the same body of laws impartially administered regulates the behavior of all people, including government officials. The law acts as a check on political power and protects the rights of both majorities and minorities. The rule of law protects the basic rights of people and does so by restraining and checking the powers of government. Equal protection of the law mandates that governments must administer the law in a uniform fashion to ensure that laws do not discriminate. Congress may impeach the president and other federal officials accused of and found guilty of improper conduct. Once removed from office, the government may prosecute individuals accused of crimes. The due process clause in the Fifth and Fourteenth amendments guarantees people certain rights including a fair and speedy trial, impartial juries, and the right to legal counsel. The courts gave interpreted clauses, due process and equal protection, to enlarge and extend basic rights. For example, in 1963, the Supreme Court ruled that courts must provide criminal defendants with legal counsel even if they cannot afford to hire one. The rule of law refers to both the law itself and the administration of law. Congress and the courts have extended the rule of law to many groups that at one time did not enjoy that protection. Delegates at the Constitutional Convention were well aware that in a monarchial form of government, the monarch could arbitrarily determine what was or was not law. Delegates at the Constitutional Convention wanted to make certain the rule of law protected against that type of arbitrary governance.

CONSTITUTIONAL PRINCIPLES: LIMITED GOVERNMENT

The 1776 Declaration of Independence was based on the idea that the government of Great Britain had infringed on the rights of the colonists by exceeding its authority and abusing its powers. The Constitution adopted in 1789 grants the government certain powers but also limits those powers. At the Constitutional Convention, a major difference between the Federalists and the anti-Federalists centered on the proposed powers for the new government. The anti-Federalists opposed ratifying the Constitution because they thought it granted too much power to the national government. The agreement to attach a Bill of Rights to the Constitution won over some opponents. It restricts government power by defining certain rights the government must respect. The Ninth Amendment protects those rights not specifically listed in the Bill of Rights. The Tenth Amendment also places limitations on the national government. In addition to the Bill of Rights, devices such as the separation of power, checks and balances, the judiciary, elections, and federalism act as a check on the government's power. How limited or expansive a government's power should be varies from one democracy to another and from one historical period to another. The national government now has much more power and responsibility than it had during the period right after the adoption of the Constitution. At the state level, the power of government is limited but the limitations vary from state to state. Republicans and Democrats often disagree about how much and what kind of power the government should have but both agree on the need for limits. The government may expand its powers in response to emergencies and unusual events. During a national emergency, a government may be permitted to do things that otherwise would be unacceptable. In 1942, President Roosevelt issued an executive order that resulted in the internment of more than 100,000 Japanese who were American citizens because they allegedly were a threat to American security. Roosevelt ordered the internment despite the fact there was no indication the Japanese-Americans threatened America in any way. When Roosevelt ordered the internment, many Japanese-Americans were serving in the armed forces and engaged in combat.

CONSTITUTIONAL PRINCIPLES: SEPARATION OF POWERS

The delegates at the Constitutional Convention believed they could help protect freedoms by separating governmental powers into three branches, executive, legislative, and judicial. One of the most prominent advocates of separated powers was the French political philosopher, Baron de Montesquieu. He influenced the thinking of James Madison who vigorously supported separating the powers of the three branches. He believed this device would effectively prevent any one group of interests from dominating the government and each branch could act as a check on the others. Delegates to the Constitutional Convention not only created three separate branches, they also made certain their powers overlapped. The president may propose legislation but the legislature must give its approval before it becomes law. If critics believe the law is unconstitutional they can take the issue to the courts. Advocates of separated powers believed the conflict that would inevitable arise between the executive and legislature would result in better legislation and greater protection from government tyranny. Article III of the Constitution created an independent judiciary although it did not grant the Supreme Court the right of judicial review. The Court assumed that right in Marbury v. Madison 1803. The Supreme Court can act as a check on government power but it has also has contributed to the expansion of government power. Delegates at the Constitutional Convention decided to adopt a federal form of government that distributes powers between the national and state governments. This is another aspect of the separation of power doctrine.

CONSTITUTIONAL PRINCIPLES: CHECKS AND BALANCES

The three branches of government have their own powers spelled out in the first three articles of the Constitution. The three branches exercise their powers within a system of checks and balances. There are formal and informal checks and balances within and between the three branches of government. Since 1860, two political parties have dominated the American political system, the Republicans and Democrats. The two parties are a part of the system of checks and balances. There are divisions within each of the parties based on such things as ideology, economics, and sectional interests. Within the executive branch of government, there is often conflict between departments over turf, access to the president, and budgetary interests. Members of the Supreme Court often disagree with each other. When they agree on a ruling, they may disagree on the reasons for it. The House and Senate check each other because both houses must approve legislation before it goes to the president. Within our federal system, there are differences between the national and state governments. There are many actors involved in the system of checks and balances including political parties, interest groups, bureaucracy, and the media. Foreign governments and organizations may also act as a check on the government's power. Other governments, international institutions such as the United Nations, and nongovernmental organizations influence American policy, both foreign and domestic. Whenever the government deals with an issue, interest groups on both sides lobby the Congress and other branches of government to advance their interests. These groups sometimes act as a check on each other.

CONSTITUTIONAL PRINCIPLES: FEDERALISM

Before the adoption of the Constitution in 1789, each state in the confederation was sovereign. Sovereignty meant they controlled most of their own affairs without interference by the national government. Delegates at the Constitutional Convention decided to adopt a federal form of government. A good definition of federalism is the constitutional distribution of power between the national and state governments. It is also another aspect of checks and balances and separated powers. The definition of federalism is simple enough but the reality is much more complex. The national government exercises some powers, state governments exercise others, and both governments share some powers such as taxation. The distribution of power at the three levels, national, state, and shared, are the delegated, reserved, and concurrent powers. The distribution of power within the federal system is dynamic and subject to change. In 1789, when the states approved the Constitution they possessed a great deal of power but this changed with the passing of time. The national government assumed more and more power vis-à-vis the states particularly after the Civil War. Some changes in the distribution of power are the result of developments since the adoption of the Constitution. There was little interstate commerce when delegates approved the Constitution but this changed as the economy grew and expanded and the means of transporting goods improved. Interstate commerce requires regulations for a variety of reasons including safety and health reasons. Although the power to regulate commerce takes up only one sentence in the Constitution, Congress and the courts can define commerce expansively to include "commercial activity." This definition enables the national government to regulate many things not usually associated with commerce including civil rights and criminal activities. Beginning in 1932, President Roosevelt's New Deal legislation further shifted the distribution of power in favor of the national government. Since 1936, many Supreme Court rulings have contributed to the increase of power at the national level. The globalization process is another factor that has enlarged the powers of the national government vis-à-vis the states. The federal system is complex because the flow of power between the national government and the states is multidirectional. Power flows in both directions concurrently.

CONSTITUTION

Constitutions may accurately or inaccurately describe the structure and functions of a government and may serve a number of different purposes. Constitutions may be relatively realistic or constructed to serve as propaganda. The Soviet Union had several constitutions that allegedly guaranteed the basic rights of the Soviet people but in fact the constitutions had nothing to do with the actual governing of the country. There were no limits on the power of the Soviet government. Governments may rite constitutions to bestow legitimacy on a government regardless of how it behaves. Great Britain has no individual document described as its constitution yet democratic principles determine how the government rules the country. The American Constitution, completed in 1787 and ratified in 1789, is misleading because of its brevity. For example, the commerce clause in Article I consists of only one sentence but in fact is the source of much governmental power. The Constitution has seven articles and numerous sections dealing with a variety of issues. All the articles and sections deal with different aspects of the governing process. Policy makers have reinterpreted parts of the Constitution as conditions have changed and values evolved. All told, the American Constitution is one of the shortest in the world and its brevity has contributed to its longevity. The Constitution deals primarily with principles rather than providing a detailed blueprint about how the government functions. Congress and the courts can interpret and reinterpret the constitutional principles to deal with changing circumstances. If necessary, the Constitution can be amended although the process is awkward and seldom used. The Supreme Court may issue decisions that alter the meaning of particular clauses of the Constitution. The quality of the Constitution is apparent in that it has remained basically intact despite the fact that when ratified the United States consisted of thirteen states, had a population of approximately three million, and had an agricultural economy. Over the years the United States developed into one of the most powerful nations in the world yet the Constitution remains basically unchanged.

ARTICLE I: CONGRESS

The Constitution is a relatively short document with only seven articles. The delegates at the Constitutional Convention decided to deal with the legislative branch in Article I because they believed it was the most important of the three branches of government and the most representative. The delegates decided on a bicameral legislature in part to deal with the problem of how best to represent the large and small states. Many southerners wanted one branch of congress to represent the states to better protect their interests in slavery. Under the Articles of Confederation, Congress consisted of only one house. At the Constitutional Convention, the delegates adopted the Connecticut compromise that satisfied the large and small states. The Senate represents states but population determines the composition of the House of Representatives. Article I, section 8, of the Constitution can be misleading because it lists only eighteen powers of Congress. These are most of the enumerated powers but Congress is not limited to just eighteen. There are also implied powers. The "necessary and proper" clause of Article I, section 8, gives Congress the power to do what is necessary and proper to carry out its duties. Over the years, this section greatly expanded the power of Congress and the national government. The necessary and proper clause was one reason why Anti-Federalists opposed ratifying the Constitution. They correctly anticipated the growing power of the national government. Article I specifically grants Congress the power to regulate interstate commerce and this too has been a significant source of power as the American economy transitioned from agriculture to an industrial base and then a postindustrial or service economy. As the economy transitioned, new powers and regulations became necessary. It is, for example, one thing for farmers to raise, kill, and sell chickens in their state. When this process involves more than one state then the national government intervenes to help ensure the entire process conforms to national standards to protect such things as health and safety. The power of the national government has also expanded as a result of the globalization process.

ARTICLE II: PRESIDENT

Article II, Section 2 of the Constitution specifically lists only six powers for the president. This is misleading. The president has enormous powers. In addition to being the most powerful politician in the country, his power extends far beyond the national borders. Some specific powers include Commander in Chief of the armed forces, negotiating treaties with the advice of the Senate, appointing ambassadors, and appointing judges to the Supreme Court and other federal courts. He is obligated to "faithfully execute" the laws of the land. The Congress and the president frequently clash regarding the powers granted to each by the Constitution because the powers overlap and there are conflicting interests making demands on the government. The conflict between the two branches is what the founding fathers intended. They wanted the two branches to check each other. The president often wins these conflicts because of his access to the media and the ability to appeal directly to the American people. The playing field is not level but it is not entirely one sided. The issues under consideration sometimes determine the power of each of the two branches. The president has the power to dispatch American military forces abroad without the approval of Congress although the exercise of this power can prove controversial. Since World War II, the president has frequently dispatched military forces abroad without consulting Congress in any meaningful way. Article I gives Congress the power to declare war but since World War II nations no longer issue such declarations. The United States has militarily intervened in many countries and fought several wars since

WW II without a declaration of war. America's rise as a superpower has greatly strengthened the power of the president. When there is a crisis or an emergency the American people look to the president, not to Congress, for leadership. Congress frequently has the upper hand when dealing with issues such as trade, government grants, and funding legislation. Another factor that influences the ebb and flow of power between the two branches of government is the president's popularity. This is an important source of power and influence. Congress is more likely to respond positively to demands made by the president if he has a high approval rating. The interesting thing about presidential power is the fact there are strong and weak presidents yet both types rule within the same Constitutional framework.

ARTICLE III: JUDICIARY

Article III of the Constitution deals with the American judicial system. It is clear the delegates to the Constitutional Convention devoted more time and attention to congress and the president than to the judicial branch. They assumed the judiciary would be the least important of the three branches and in many ways would resemble the British judicial system. Article III does not specifically grant the Supreme Court the right to declare acts of Congress unconstitutional. The Supreme Court assumed that power in Marbury v. Madison 1803. From the time of the Marbury ruling until 1858, the Court did not declare any other acts of Congress unconstitutional. The Constitution established the office of chief justice of the Supreme Court but Congress determines the number of judges that serve. Since 1869, the Court has had nine judges. The Supreme Court has original and appellate jurisdictions. An example of original jurisdiction would be a conflict between the president and the Congress or a conflict between the states that requires adjudication. The appellate jurisdiction allows the Supreme Court to review decisions made by lower courts.

Congress also decides on the establishment of district courts with original jurisdiction and intermediate appellate courts. Congress may also create inferior courts such as the United States Tax Court and U.S. Court of Appeals for Veteran Claims. Article III also deals with the question of treason. The Constitution makes it difficult to find someone guilty of treason because many delegates attending the Constitutional Convention had engaged in acts of treason against the British government. Some Supreme Court decisions such as the 1858 Dred Scott ruling or the 1954 Brown v. Board of Education ruling had a profound impact on life in America. The Supreme Court has developed in ways not anticipated by those attending the Constitutional Convention. They never assumed the Court would develop into such a powerful institution. James Madison thought the judiciary would be the "least dangerous" branch of government.

ARTICLE IV

Article IV of the Constitution has four sections including the "full faith and credit" clause, the guarantee of a "republican" form of government, the "Privileges and Immunity" clause and the process for admitting new states into the union. The "full faith and credit" clause requires states to recognize such things as the public records and judicial decisions of other states. If a court finds an individual guilty of a crime and the criminal flees to another state, it is obligated to return the criminal to the original state. The guarantee of a "republican" form of government prevents states from adopting a non-democratic form of government although there is no indication of what such a government would look like. The "Privileges and Immunity" clause prevents states from discriminating against individuals from other states. Article IV also spells out the procedure for admitting new states into the union. This provision was last used in 1959 to admit Hawaii and Alaska as states.

ARTICLE V

The amendatory process is located in Article V of the Constitution. Delegates at the Constitutional Convention saw the need for possible amendments in the future but they made the amendatory process difficult because they wanted to avoid having to deal with frivolous amendments. The Constitution has been amended twenty seven times including the first ten amendments. Two amendments, XVIII and XXI, deal with the same subject, prohibition. There are two ways to amend the Constitution and each involves a two-stage process. (1) Congress may propose an amendment by a two-thirds vote in each house or (2) two-thirds of the state legislatures request Congress to convene a national convention to propose amendments. Congress has never used the second process because it would not control such a convention. After Congress approves a proposed amendment, states may ratify it in either of two ways: (1) three-fourths of the state legislatures must approve the amendment or (2) states convene special conventions to vote on the proposed amendment. Either method requires a majority vote for approval. The Constitution has been amended relatively few times because the brevity of the Constitution permits flexibility. Changes in the way the government functions have come about without necessarily resorting to the amendatory process.

ARTICLE VI

Among other things, Article VI makes the Constitution the "supreme law of the land." The supremacy clause was included in the Constitution to correct a major defect in the Articles of Confederation that allowed states to ignore those national laws they did not wish to obey. Delegates convened the Constitutional Convention to create a system of government that permitted the national government to have more powers than it had under the Articles. There were basically only two groups represented at the Constitutional Convention, those that wanted to strengthen the confederation and those that wanted to eliminate it. Those opposed to modifying the Articles boycotted the convention.

ARTICLE VII

This article deals with the process for ratifying the Constitution. Nine states had to ratify the Constitution before it went into effect. New Hampshire, the ninth state, ratified the Constitution in June 1788. New York and Virginia were not among the first nine states to ratify the Constitution but they did so shortly after the New Hampshire vote. Failure of either state to ratify the Constitution would have seriously compromised the entire process. The viability of the Union required their participation. The Constitution became operative in 1789.

CONGRESS

A BICAMERAL LEGISLATURE

The U.S. Congress is a bicameral legislature meaning it is composed of two bodies, the House and Senate. A bicameral legislature was one solution to the representation issue at the Constitutional Convention. The issue involved the power of big and small states. Under the Articles, the thirteen states were all equal. The Continental Congress was a unicameral body. Each state had one vote regardless of geographical size or population. At the Constitutional Convention, the small states feared losing their power. The compromise between the big and small states, the Connecticut Compromise, also known as the Great Compromise, resulted in the creation of a bicameral legislature, one house with representation based on population, the other representing states. Without this compromise enough states would have refused to ratify the Constitution thus guaranteeing its defeat. One disadvantage of a bicameral legislature is the duplication that occurs and the time members of the executive branch spend appearing before congressional committees. If the Secretary of State addresses a committee in the House, he or she will probably have to do the same in the Senate if both committees have the same jurisdiction. Committees in each house often go over the same material and have the same concerns. On some issues, the secretary may have to address more than one committee and this too may occur in both houses. One argument in favor of bicameralism is that duplication enables more scrutiny of proposed legislation allegedly providing more opportunities to improve its quality. Bicameralism intentionally slows the legislative process. Both houses must approve all legislation. If the two houses pass different versions of a bill, differences must be reconciled before they send the legislation to the president for his approval or veto. If different political parties control each house of Congress the reconciliation process can be contentious. Getting congressional approval for a bill is a slow process that must successfully navigate through pass many veto points. Congress is a deliberative body thus the legislative process takes time. Congress carries out several functions but its primary function is to represent the people. There are different interpretations as to how Congress should do this. Should members of Congress simply reflect public opinion back home or should members filter and interpret the thinking of constituents. Congress has an oversight function to make certain executive departments properly implements approved legislation. The oversight function is a part of the system of checks and balances. Members of Congress also carry out constituent services.

HOUSE OF REPRESENTATIVES

The House of Representatives has 435 members, elected for two-year terms, representing congressional districts. The numerical size of the House has varied over time depending on changes in the population. As the population increased, it became necessary to increase the number of representatives but this process is not automatic. When the House of Representatives first convened in 1789 membership numbered sixty-five. In 1913, Congress increased its membership to four hundred and thirty five. It has not changed since then. Some critics think the House should increase its membership to better represent the diversity of the population. The population in

1913 was less than one hundred million. The population is now more than three hundred million. Most members of the House are white males but minority and female membership continues to increase. In 2009, Democrats elected Nancy Pelosi as Speaker of the House, the first women to hold that position. The Speaker is the most powerful leadership position in the House and is second in line to succeed the president should he die in office or become incapacitated. The House and Senate share certain powers but each also has distinct powers. Powers exclusive to the House include initiation of revenue bills, impeaching officials, and electing the president when no candidate wins a majority of Electoral College votes. In addition to passing legislation, members of the House also have an oversight function. This involves determining how the executive branch implements legislation to make certain its purpose is not compromised. Oversight is a part of the system of checks and balances. The House will often be more diligent in carrying out its oversight function if the opposition party controls the White House. The House, by a two-thirds vote, may decide to over-ride a presidential veto but the Senate must concur also with at least a two-thirds vote. If a constituent has a problem such as a late social security check or a disputed claim to a service, the member of the House is usually eager to have someone on his staff investigate and correct the problem. Constituent services help members win reelection. House members spend a good deal of time fund raising. Running for Congress has become increasingly expensive. Some critics believe the high cost of running for office enables groups with substantial financial assets to have undue influence. The average cost of running a campaign to win a House seat is about one million dollars. The minimum age for House members is twenty-five. Candidates must be citizens for at least seven years, and must reside in the state where the district is located but need not live in the district. Most House members do live in the district they represent. The one exception to this rule in recent years is Allen West. He did not live in the district that voted him into office in 2010. He is a rare exception to this political rule. Some states have passed laws requiring candidates to live in the district they wish to represent.

SENATE

The Senate has one hundred members that serve a six year term. Each state, regardless of its geographical size or population, has two senators. Political observers sometimes refer to the Senate as a club because members are more likely to know each other because of their frequent contacts. This is much less true in the House. One third of the Senate is up for election every two years. This enables the Senate to act as a check on the president's power. A victor in a presidential race means that however popular he may be when elected, two-thirds of the Senators did not participate in the election. Current public opinion or the popularity of the newly elected president may not influence the sitting Senators previously elected. Unlike the House, members of the Senate may serve on more than one important congressional committee. Senators usually represent multiple interests because they represent states rather than districts. This sometime gives them more flexibility in deciding how to vote on a particular bill compared to House members. The Senate has some unique powers. It must approve many presidential appointments and has the power to ratify treaties. It may, by a two-thirds vote, remove federal officials from office including the president. Senators can stage a filibuster to prevent, delay, or modify proposed legislation. The House does not have this power. The Senate, similar to the House, carries out oversight functions. The media often pays more attention to members of the Senate compared to House members because of the difference in the size of each house. Senators often appear on television more than their House counterparts. Presidential candidates often select members of the Senate for running mates. Some Senators that became vice president include Alben Barkley, Harry Truman, Richard Nixon,

Lyndon Johnson, Hubert Humphrey, Walter Mondale, Dan Quayle, Al Gore, and Joe Biden. Some Senators acquire presidential ambitions. Presidents Obama, Nixon, Johnson, Kennedy, and Truman served in the Senate before getting to the White House. Other senators have sought the presidential nomination but failed. The list includes Barkley, Quale, and Biden. Senators serve for a six year term. Candidates must be at least thirty years of age, be a citizen, and reside in the state he or she wants to represent.

CONGRESS: COMMITTEE SYSTEM

Committees and subcommittees do much of the legislative work in Congress. The committee system helps expedite the legislative process and enables members to develop expertise because each committee has a defined jurisdiction. Members usually remain on a committee for a prolonged period to buildup expertise, seniority, and power. The chair of a committee is ordinarily the member of the majority party with the most seniority on the committee. The Republican Party limits the tenure of committee chairs to six years. The Democratic Party has no term limits for chairs. Each party makes its own rules regarding eligibility for chairs and the length of time they serve. The House has a Rules Committee that controls the legislative process. It determines how much time members may debate a bill and which, if any, amendments it will allow. Unlike the Senate, the House tightly regulates time for debates because of the size of the institution. Members of Congress often try to get on committees that will help them win reelection. A member of the House or a Senator from a basically agricultural state will try to get on committees dealing with agriculture. Committee members try to make certain the government awards contracts to companies or corporations in their state or district. Congressional committees contribute to the fragmentation of Congress and the fragmentation sometimes makes it difficult to hold Congress responsible for what it does or does not do. Different committees and subcommittees may kill a bill or amend it beyond recognition. Members may approve a bill they dislike knowing it will die somewhere along the legislative process. Member may do this if the measure is popular with constituents back home. The committee system helps lobbyists influence Congress. Lobbyists may rely on one committee or subcommittee or a particular chairperson to help pass or defeat legislation.

CONGRESS: TYPES OF COMMITTEES

There are four types of committees: standing (also called permanent), joint, temporary, and conference. The House of Representatives has twenty-three permanent committees; the Senate has sixteen. Due to the difference in size of membership, House committees have more members than those in the Senate. Unlike the House, Senators may serve on more than one important committee. Committees expedite the legislative process. They hear expert testimony and provide interest groups and interested parties with an opportunity to influence pending legislation. Most bills that become law must go through the committee system. By the time a bill gets to the floor of the House or the Senate, the final vote is usually predictable. Most committees cover a particular subject matter but some, such as the Rules Committee in the House, deal with the legislative process. Committees that deal with money appropriations are particularly important given the size of the national budget. Deciding how money is spent, who spends it, and for what purpose are subjects of interest to all members of Congress. Money is a source of influence and power. Committees dealing with military and defense issues influence budgetary priorities because they are a large part of the national budget. Defense spending can have a significant impact on employment in a state or a congressional district.

CONGRESSIONAL SENIORITY

Congressional seniority is a major source of political power. The number of years a member serves in Congress often determines committee assignments. Some committees are more desirable than others. Time on a committee is source of power because seniority usually determines the chair of a committee and the ranking minority member. Committee chairs influence whether legislation will be approved and in what form. Details can be vitally important in the final version of a bill. Seniority enables members to develop a degree of expertise on whatever subjects fall under a committee's jurisdiction. Senior members of a committee often give policy continuity and coherence because of their expertise and experience. Committees can evaluate legislative proposals made by the executive branch and may recommend amendments to improve its quality. Members of Congress with seniority are better able to access decision makers in the executive branch of government and this may help promote more cooperation between the two branches. Critics of seniority point out that it ignores capabilities and individual competence. Individuals with seniority often represent safe electoral districts with little political party competition. The seniority system has the advantage of eliminating competition to become chair and it eliminates the need for dispensing favors to win votes. Democrats in the House rely on seniority to a greater degree than the Republicans.

HOW A BILL BECOMES A LAW

The legislative process seems to be simple enough but in fact the process is quiet complicated. Proposed legislation must survive a number of hurdles before becoming law. Legislation may come to an abrupt end in either house of Congress, in a committee, or a subcommittee. The president may veto a bill or the Supreme Court may rule it unconstitutional. Individual members of Congress familiar with the complicated rules may use those rules to kill bills or slow the legislative process. Then there is the question of how a bureaucracy will implement a bill. As a proposed bill goes through the legislative process members may amend it beyond recognition. All legislative proposals, regardless of where they originate, must have a congressional sponsor. Members of Congress may propose legislation for basically political reasons without any expectation of legislative approval. Legislative proposals may come from several sources. Two of the most important are the executive branch and individual members of Congress. When a member introduces a bill, in either house, it then goes to a committee for consideration. Usually, it will then go to the appropriate subcommittee. It may conduct hearings and invite opponents and **supporters of the legislation to testify. If approved, the legislation then goes to the full committee and it repeats the same process. If both chambers approve the legislation, it then goes to the president for his signature or veto. Congress, by a two-thirds vote may override a presidential veto. If the House and Senate pass different versions of a bill, it then goes to a conference committee composed of members of both houses. If the conference committee approves a bill, it then goes back to the House and Senate for another vote before going to the president for his approval or veto. There are many veto points in the legislative process thus it is easier to kill legislation than to win passage.**

PRESIDENT: CENTERPIECE OF THE AMERICAN SYSTEM

Although most people cannot name their representatives in Congress, most know the name of the president. He is the centerpiece of the American political system. There are several reasons for this.

The Congress is a complex institution difficult to understand because of its size, structure, bicameralism, and political culture. Much congressional work is shielded from public view. There are always several leaders with competing viewpoints who claim to speak for the institution. Members of the same political party may have conflicting views. One individual occupies the presidency with almost unlimited access to the media. When he addresses the American people, he does so alone or with individuals sharing his policy preferences. The people look to him for guidance and reassurance during a time of crisis. As the powers of the national government increased so too did the powers of the president. If there is a major crisis, people expect him to offer solutions. He almost always has multiple major problems he must try to resolve on an immediate basis. He can also dominate the media when there is no crisis and he is simply carrying out routine functions such as meeting another head of state, attending an international conference, or presiding over a state dinner. If an athletic team wins a major national or international event, it can expect a congratulatory message from the president. He can use television to address the nation to explain a policy or deal with an emergency. Some voters view the president as being above partisan politics because he is the only nationally elected leader, however, his policy preferences reflect the values associated with his political party although his rhetoric may try to conceal this. It is sometimes difficult to reconcile the president's role as party leader and his role as spokesman for the nation. Presidents almost always claim that the policies they support are good for the entire nation or at least a majority of the people. This is particularly true when the president is campaigning for a second term.

PRESIDENTIAL ROLES

The president has many roles and sometimes they conflict with each other. The Constitution determines some roles and others have developed as a result of changing political circumstances. The president's roles include head of state, head of government, chief diplomat, head of his party, commander and chief and chief legislator. The president is the head of state and in that role he represents all the American people. This role is similar to that of the monarchy in Great Britain. The monarch is not associated with any political party or government policies. The president has a second role as chief executive or head of government. In this role he is the political leader of the country. His political party affiliation helps shape his policy recommendations. He makes many appointments to staff the offices of government including members of his cabinet and judges at the federal level. He usually appoints individuals that share his values and policy preferences. He is also responsible for executing the laws of the land. In his State of the Union message, he lays out his legislative priorities for Congress to consider. As the head of his political party, he promotes party policies and often participates in the electoral process to help elect or reelect members of his party. When a president visits a foreign country he does so as the head of state, head of government, chief diplomat, and leader of his party. The roles are often difficult to separate. When President Nixon visited China and the Soviet Union in 1972, his visits received worldwide attention and undoubtedly contributed to his overwhelming victory in the 1972 presidential election. The president, for a variety of reasons, may lose the confidence of the American people. President Nixon was overwhelming reelected in 1972 but resigned in 1974 rather than face impeachment charges. The most serious charge against Nixon was that he abused his powers and repeatedly lied to members of his party. He decided to resign when he learned that Republican members of Congress were going to vote in favor of impeachment. Although presidents may become unpopular, they almost always enjoy a higher approval rating than Congress. The president is the centerpiece of the American political system.

PRESIDENT'S CABINET

President Washington established the cabinet during his first term in office. It consisted of the Vice President, Secretary of State, Secretary of Treasury, Secretary of War, Attorney General, and the Postmaster General. There is no mention of a cabinet in the Constitution but the president needs advisors to help cope with the many problems confronting the government. The voters do not expect the president to be knowledgeable about all the problems he must deal with thus the need for trusted advisors. The president's cabinet has many functions including giving advice to the president, managing government agencies, and making certain the president's policies are carried out. The cabinet now consists of fifteen members including the vice president. The most important cabinet secretaries are ordinarily those in charge of the State Department, the Department of Defense, and the Justice Department. The importance of the cabinet office depends on current problems and the president's relations with individual members. In cabinet meetings, tradition dictates that members be seated in a hierarchal order. The president often prefers meeting with particular individuals rather than the entire cabinet because most issues are not relevant to some cabinet offices. If the president is dealing with a major policy issue he will consult with individual cabinet members but he may also consult with outsiders because of their expertise and experience. In addition to advising the president, cabinet secretaries must make certain the institutions they are in charge of function properly. They must frequently testify before congressional committees and this usually requires a good deal of preparation. They must justify budget requests, defend policies, and deflect criticism. Cabinet secretaries must sometimes meet representatives of the media to explain administration policies and respond to criticisms. They must also deal with the many interest groups that want to influence government policies. These groups often have conflicting interests the secretary must try to reconcile. Members of Congress sometimes pressure departments to initiate policies opposed by the president. Cabinet secretaries need a variety of political skills to effectively deal with many cross pressures.

SELECTION OF CABINET MEMBERS

The president elect usually has a long list of individuals wishing to head cabinet departments. In selecting cabinet members, the president considers an individual's skills, experience, knowledge of how Washington works, personality, and ability to get along with others. The president may rely on trusted friends to make recommendations. Politics is almost always a factor in the selection process. The president will usually select individuals associated with his political party although he may appoint people because of other factors, including a desire to appear non-partisan or bipartisan. The president may wish to select individuals familiar with the department he or she will lead. The president may also seek to balance such things as gender, geography, race, ethnicity, and ideology. The president determines the frequency of cabinet meetings. Some cabinet members such as the Secretary of State or the Secretary of Defense meet with the president on a regular and sometimes a daily basis. One of the unusual features of American politics is that the president may not have had a personal relationship with individuals he selects to serve. He may select an individual to serve because he or she represents an important political constituency. When appointing cabinet officials, the president must be confident the individual will be able to cope with the many demands made by members of Congress and other constituencies. Cabinet secretaries must appear before congressional committees and these meetings can be quite contentious. Cabinet secretaries sometimes have a dual loyalty that may cause friction with the president. They must carry out the president's policies, be responsive to the department they rule, and sensitive to the demands of interest groups even though they may disagree with the president's policies. All these pressures contribute to the fact that secretaries rarely remain in office for four years. There are a number of other reasons for this as well. Some cabinet members are not Washington insiders nor are they necessarily interested in a political career. Cabinet members that come from the private sector are often eager to return to that sector after a brief tour in Washington. Those appointed to serve in the cabinet often do so for much less money than they could earn in the private sector. There is also the fact that running a large government bureaucracy is a difficult, time-consuming job. Secretaries frequently work a seven-day week and a fourteen to eighteen hour day. This not only puts a lot of pressure on the secretary but also on his or her family. There are numerous reasons for cabinet turnovers including the combined pressure of reduced income, long hours, travels around the country or to foreign countries, and neglect of family. At times, cabinet members get frustrated because of the difficulty of getting things done in Washington. A cabinet secretary may issue an order that subordinates may or may not carry out.

INFORMAL CABINET

The president sometimes relies on individuals outside the government for advice and recommendations. At other times, he may rely on someone with a formal position in the government to offer advice on a wide range of topics or problems. President Kennedy appointed his brother Robert Kennedy as Attorney General but he advised the president on numerous issues not always related to the functions of his office. Robert Kennedy, for example, was a major part of the decision making process dealing with the 1962 Cuban missile crisis. At times, the president may rely on one particular individual for assistance and advice. Harry Hopkins was Secretary of Commerce from 1938 to 1940 but he was in fact one of Roosevelt's most trusted advisors from the time of his election in 1932. He sought Hopkins' advice on a variety of issues including foreign policy. He had much more influence on the making of foreign policy than did the Secretary of State. During World War II, Hopkins dealt extensively with Great Britain's Prime Minister Churchill and Marshal Stalin, leader of the Soviet Union. Members of Roosevelt's staff often referred to Hopkins aopkins was sometimes referreds the "Deputy President." The president may call on people outside the government for advice. These individuals generally have extensive experience dealing with the way Washington works and do not have a political agenda that conflicts with the president's policy preferences. They are simply "Washington insiders" the president relies on for confidential, objective advice. They know how Washington works. There are also advantages in relying on outsiders for advice. They are not officially a part of the government and therefore need not appear before congressional committees to answer questions about the president's policies nor do they have to respond to the media.

JUDICIARY

JUDICIARY ACT 1789

In 1789, Congress approved the Judiciary Act establishing the American federal court system composed of three tiers, the Supreme Court, Appellate Courts, and district courts. Each of the three tiers has its own jurisdiction. Delegates at the 1787 Constitutional Convention did not devote much attention to the judicial system. They thought it would be the least important of the three branches of government. Article III established the Supreme Court but delegates said little about its composition, membership, or jurisdiction. That duty fell to the first Congress that met in 1789. Congress determines the number of courts, both trial and appellate, and determines the number of Supreme Court judges. Initially the Supreme Court had six judges but since 1869, there have been nine judges. George Washington appointed John Jay the first Chief Justice. The 1789 Judiciary Act created the office of Attorney General. The Anti-Federalists wanted to limit the number of courts and their jurisdiction. They wanted the court system to be primarily under the control of the states, not the national government. They disliked the idea of appointing judges rather than have them elected and they also opposed life tenure. They feared a strong judicial system would endanger individual rights because judges would be appointed, not elected. Anti-Federalists preferred a weak federal judicial system but they lost the battle. The Judiciary Act did not give the Supreme Court the power judicial review but the court assumed that power in Marbury v. Madison 1803.

SUPREME COURT

At the 1787 Constitutional Convention, delegates established the Supreme Court but did not give it the power to declare an act of Congress unconstitutional. The Supreme Court has both original and appellate jurisdictions. Original jurisdiction call for the court to resolves conflicts such as those involving the president and Congress, between two or more states, and disputes between states and the national government. Resolving differences between the states and the national government is an important court function because how power is distributed between the two levels of government if often a contentious issue involving constitutional questions. Federalism requires an arbiter because the flow of power between the two levels is constantly changing. The division of power between the national and state governments was a major issue at the Constitutional Convention and it generated a good deal of debate. In 1789, the state governments had much more power than the national government but this changed because of changing political and economic conditions and various Supreme Court rulings such as McCulloch v. Maryland (1819), Brown v. Board of Education (1954), and Roe v. Wade (1973). After 1936, the Supreme Court frequently supported the expansion of power by the national government that it had rejected in the past. This reversal was made possible by the fact several Supreme Court judges retired thus enabling President Roosevelt to appoint new judges that shared his political philosophy. They approved New Deal legislation that contributed to the growth of government power at the national level. In some instances, the Supreme Court seeks to bring uniformity to the federal process but it also seeks to protect diversity. A good example of this is the question of capital punishment. Some states have capital punishment, others do not. The Supreme Court seeks to make certain the states that permit capital punishment institute uniform procedures for its implementation. Most Supreme Court cases involve the appellate process. The court reviews decisions made by lower courts. Appellate courts may decide similar cases differently and the differences need to be reconciled. Before the Supreme Court puts a case on the docket, four judges (rule of four) must agree to hear the case. Each year, the court receives thousands of requests to hear cases but accepts relatively few, approximately one hundred a year. The actual number varies from year to year.

SUPREME COURT: SELECTING JUDGES

One of the most important presidential powers is nominating judges for the federal court system, particularly the Supreme Court. Although there are few formal requirements for such appointments, many factors influence the selection process including experience, party identification, judicial temperament, and political party control of the Senate. Non-governmental organizations such as the American Bar Association may play an important role in the selection of nominees and the confirmation process. Presidents usually have a list of individuals to choose from should a vacancy on the court occur. Members of the president's staff thoroughly evaluate potential candidates before compiling a final list. Presidents want to be prepared should a vacancy suddenly occur. The confirmation process can be contentious. The Senate has rejected about twenty percent of the president's choices. The process may be less contentious if the same political party controls the presidency and the Senate. The president must choose carefully because judges can only be removed from office by the impeachment process. The House of Representatives has impeached two judges, John Pickering and Samuel Chase, but only Pickering was removed from office. In 1969, Abe Fortas resigned from the Supreme Court because of a financial scandal and the possibility of impeachment. In addition to his financial problems, critics accused Fortas of offering President Johnson advice on political issues. Regardless of how thoroughly the White House vets a candidate for a Supreme Court appointment there is no guarantee the justice will vote in a particular way on a given issue. Once confirmed by the Senate, justices serve for life and this helps insulate them from political pressures. Some policy makers think there should be a mandatory retirement age. If a justice becomes mentally impaired, it is not clear how he or she could be compelled to retire other than through the impeachment process.

SUPREME COURT: HOW JUDGES VOTE

How Supreme Court judges vote depends on many factors. They must consider things such as precedents (stare decisis), the meaning of the law, popular opinion, political factors, and the impact of their decisions. Justices may influence each other. The chief justice can sometimes play a particularly important role in influencing how his colleagues vote. Justices realize that decisions may have significant political consequences although they may not anticipate all of them. This makes the deliberative process all the more important. The 1858 Dred Scott decision helped bring about the civil war. The 1954 Brown v. Bd. of Education case ended legally sanctioned segregation and revolutionized race relations in America. In that case, Chief Justice Warren managed to construct a unanimous decision and this helped insulate the court from the widespread criticism directed at it from many sections of the country but particularly from the South. The unanimous vote was important because the Chief Justice was well aware of the historic importance of the issue. Between 1932 and 1936, the Supreme Court was controversial because it invalidated much New Deal legislation attempting to deal with the consequences of the 1929 economic crash. After President Roosevelt's overwhelming victory in the 1936 presidential election, the court began to validate New Deal programs and policies. Judges allegedly are objective in arriving at their opinions but obviously political beliefs, values, and public opinion influence how they vote. Presidents do not appoint judges if their judicial or political opinions suggest their values and beliefs are different from those of the president but there is no sure way of determining how a judge will vote after the Senate confirms the nominee. President Eisenhower appointed Earl Warren as Chief Justice but subsequently regretted the appointment. Eisenhower said appointing Warren was the biggest mistake he ever made. Although labeling judges liberal or conservative is somewhat subjective, the fact is that some judges consistently vote along liberal or conservative lines.

APPELLATE COURTS

There are thirteen appellate courts that review cases by lower courts, the trial courts. Appellate courts deal with questions of law and the facts of the case. They are concerned with the legal process, the decision-making process at the lower court level, but not necessarily with the decision itself. The Supreme Court is also an appellate court. A legal case may begin at the trial level and then be reviewed by one of the appellate courts. The Supreme Court may then review the case. Anyone losing a case at the trial level has the right of appeal to an appellate court but the court reserves the right to determine whether it will hear the case or not. At the Supreme Court level, four judges must agree to have the entire court hear a case. This is the "rule of four." Congress determines the number of judges for each circuit court. The number usually reflects the population and geographical area served by the court. There is a natural connection between the Supreme Court and the appellate courts because both deal with the appellate process. The president selects appellate court judges who must then win Senate confirmation. Some appellate court judges are put on the list of potential appointees to the Supreme Court should a vacancy occur. The record of an appellate judge enables a president to help determine the judicial outlook of a potential nominee. Both supporters and opponents scan the public record to find evidence to support or oppose the nominee. There is also the fact the Senate confirms appellate judges thus they are familiar with the confirmation process and know what to expect if appointed to the Supreme Court.

DISTRICT COURTS

There are now ninety-four district courts, also called trial courts, in the fifty states. They deal with civil and criminal cases. The number of courts in each state depends on the size of its population and the number of cases they hear. California, Texas, and New York each have four district courts. The president appoints federal trial judges who must then obtain Senate confirmation that requires a majority vote. Trial judges are often active in either of the two major parties. Members of the Senate, if they are in the same political party as the president, expect to be consulted in the naming of trial court judges if the individual lives in the Senator's state. Senators may submit names they want the president to consider when a vacancy occurs. If the president and a Senator belong to the same political party, the Senator may prevent a vote on the president's nominee if the Senator opposes the nominee from his or her state. This is the tradition of "Senatorial courtesy." If, for example, the president selects a nominee from Texas, he should consult with the Senators from that state if they are members of the president's political party. If the Senate confirms a nominee, that person serves for life unless he or she does something illegal or unethical. Congress has the right to remove federal judges from office through the impeachment process.

Political Parties

DEVELOPMENT OF POLITICAL PARTIES

The Constitution makes no mention of political parties. Many members attending the 1787 Constitutional Convention opposed political parties in part because they allegedly represented "factions" rather than the general interests of the country. Political parties developed naturally because people supporting the same cause or the same policies and sharing the same beliefs inevitably bond together. Despite the misgivings of the founding fathers, political parties became important as links between the people and the government. They are also an important instrument for organizing the government. American political parties organized around a set of beliefs defined in a general way. Voters generally identify the Democratic Party with a more liberal approach to government than the Republican Party. The latter is more conservative and less trusting of government institutions and government sponsored policies. The American political system generally operates within the two party system—the Republican and Democratic parties. One party may control one or both branches of government, the legislative and the executive. The other party then functions as the loyal opposition. Although the two parties are distinct, both must appeal to the center of the American electorate for support. State legislators are undermining the need to appeal to the center of the political electorate by creating "safe" electoral districts.

Candidates in safe districts tend to be more ideological than those in competitive districts and less willing to compromise. Ideological parties have difficulty appealing to the middle of the electorate because they tend to be more exclusive than inclusive and thus have less appeal to the average voter. Without political parties, democratic governments would not function as they do. Although the party system has been functioning for a long time, the Founding Fathers were at least partially right in their criticism. Political parties sometimes decide on policies the public supports even though they may be detrimental to the national interest in the long run. They do this in anticipation of receiving a larger proportion of the popular vote. What is good for one or both parties is not necessarily good for the country. A good example of this is the problem of entitlement programs and the growing national debt. Once people begin to receive benefits from the government, they are reluctant to accept efforts to curb costs or reduce benefits. Even if the national debt is a problem, voters will almost always support additional benefits even though such benefits may add to the debt problem. Voters do not elect or reelect politicians that promish to diminish or eliminate benefits voters cherish.

POLITICAL PARTIES: FUNCTIONS

Political parties in a democratic political system have many important functions. The primary purpose of a viable political party in a democracy is to win enough support through the electoral system to organize the government. This function is what differentiates political parties from interest groups. The latter attempt to influence government polices but they do not organize the government. Political parties, especially those in opposition, attempt to influence policies in both positive and negative ways. They help shape public opinion and if successful, they may succeed in killing or modifying policies the government favors. They may also formulate policy alternatives to give voters a choice. Political parties promote participation in the political system. This may take the form of getting out the vote, organizing demonstrations, mobilizing campaigns to influence legislation, and selecting, promoting, or supporting candidates. Parties help define the issues and play an essential role in conducting elections. They are also the instrument for transferring power. Changing governments in non-democratic systems is often the result of a coup d'état that may result in much bloodshed and violence. In democratic systems, the transfer of power is generally a peaceful process. If an individual in America is politically ambitious, joining a political party is imperative. Voters generally do not elect independents. For many voters, their only contact with the government is through a member of either political party.

TWO PARTY SYSTEM

Ever since the Civil War, two political parties, the Democratic Party and the Republican Party, have dominated the American political system. Two factors contribute to the strength of the two party system. One is the single member district. Voters may elect only one individual to represent each congressional district. The second factor is plurality voting. It enables a candidate to be elected by winning the most votes even if that does not add up to more than fifty-one percent of the vote. The victor need win only a plurality of the voters, more votes than anyone else. Third party candidates rarely receive enough votes to win an election. They usually take votes away from one of the two major parties thus contributing to the victory of the other party. Liberal third party candidates generally hurt the Democratic Party. Conservative third party candidates generally hurt the Republican Party. Third party candidates do not win many elections but they can play an important part in the electoral process. In the 2000 presidential election, Ralph Nader won enough votes in Florida to enable George

W. Bush to win the state and the election. The purpose of some third party candidates is to punish the candidate of one of the two major parties. Third party candidates may also promote a cause or a policy in the hope of making it more attractive sometime in the future. If a third party succeeds in making a policy more legitimate and popular, one of the two major political parties may adopt that cause or policy. Some policies initially promoted by third parties that eventually became law after being adopted by one or both political parties include laws dealing with child labor, health care, and racial equality. America's political culture is a major factor supporting the two party system. If voters are dissatisfied with one of the political parties they will vote for the other party or just stay home. The two party system is a major source of stability in the American political system.

TERMS—DEFINITIONS—EVENTS

AFFIRMATIVE ACTION

Affirmative action policies benefit specific groups of people based on such things as ethnicity, race, or gender. Members of these groups receive preferential treatment because of real or alleged discrimination in the past. Government agencies may apply affirmative action policies to employment, job promotions, admission to colleges and universities, graduate schools, medical and law schools, and other institutions. The policies have several goals including promoting diversity and correcting past wrongs. Opponents of affirmative action believe such policies are unfair and discriminatory, ignore merit, and promote intolerance. They do not see the justice in giving people preferential treatment now because of wrongs that occurred to past generations. Affirmative action is often associated with identity politics. Supporters of affirmative action argue that such policies simply redress grievances that have a long history but opponents claim it promotes preferential treatment and is therefore a form of reverse discrimination. Affirmative action divides those who believe in equality of opportunity from those supporting equality of results. The complexity of affirmative action policies and their broad scope has divided the Supreme Court justices. Two states, California and Washington, have abolished state affirmative action programs. Other states are considering such a ban but affirmative action programs have much support.

AGENDA SETTING

Agenda setting is an important process that helps determine policy priorities. It is a source of power as well as a manifestation of it. Presidential candidates attempt to have their priorities dominate the presidential primaries and the presidential election itself. Forcing your opponents to concentrate on your agenda can help determine electoral outcomes. Topics usually favor one side more than the other. A candidate that sets the election agenda forces opponents to discuss issues they may prefer to ignore or minimize. Certain issues have traditionally favored one political party or the other. The Republican Party prefers to emphasize security and foreign policy issues. Democrats prefer economic and social issues. This alignment does not always hold true. In the 2008 presidential election, many voters cast their ballots for Barak Obama, a Democrat, because they disapproved of President George W. Bush's foreign policies including the war in Iraq. The president enjoys a distinctive advantage in agenda setting by virtue of his access to the media. The annual State of the Union address is a useful presidential tool because it receives so much media attention in the United States and abroad. The president may also give speeches, hold news conferences, and appear at special events to promote his agenda and that of his party. He may also lobby members of Congress particularly those in his political party. Agenda setting is an important political tool because control of the agenda often determines control over issues and the terms of debate. Just getting the media to discuss whether an issue should be on the agenda may help get it there. The outcome of congressional elections helps determine the legislative agenda that often reflects the wishes of the voters supporting the majority party. The media plays a significant role in determining political agendas. There are now multiple media outlets, many more than in the past, and they reflect different viewpoints. Despite the diversity, the media will frequently concentrate on one or two issues and this ensures national attention. In the 2012 presidential election, the Republican Party emphasized the economy and the need for change. The Democratic Party emphasized the need for continuity. Presidential candidates, other than the incumbents, almost always embrace the theme of change despite the fact that bringing about significant change is always difficult to achieve. President Kennedy, after being in power for a year, said that what surprised him most about his first year in office was the difficulty of getting things done. There are always powerful forces supporting the status quo. There are many veto points in the legislative process. It is almost always easier to prevent the passage of legislation than to win approval.

ALIEN AND SEDITION ACTS

In 1789, the Federalist controlled Congress passed four acts, collectively known as the Alien and Sedition Acts. Their purpose was to stifle criticism of American policies by the Democratic Republicans led by Thomas Jefferson. He and his followers were sympathetic to France then at war with Great Britain. France helped the United States win the Revolutionary War against the hated British. Jefferson thought the United States should do more to help the French win their war. President John Adams and the Federalists were unsympathetic to the pro-French sentiment of the Democratic Republicans. In response to the criticism leveled by Jefferson and his supporters, Congress passed the Alien and Sedition Acts. Federalists accused opponents of advocating policies that would weaken the United State and might involve the country in a European war. The Alien and Sedition Acts were unpopular with the American people regardless of party affiliation. Critics claimed the acts violated the Constitution and the Tenth Amendment. The government charged a number of individuals with violating the Alien and Seditions Acts. The courts found some defendants guilty of violating the acts and they were imprisoned. When Jefferson became president in 1801, he pardoned all individuals convicted on the basis of the acts. He believed all four acts were unconstitutional but the issue never reached the U.S. Supreme Court. It had not yet assumed the power of declaring an act of Congress unconstitutional. Whenever the United States is involved in a major crisis with another country, some individuals and groups will equate dissent with a lack of patriotism. The Alien and Sedition acts contributed to the demise of the Federalist Party. It soon ceased to exist.

AMENDATORY PROCESS

The first ten amendments, the Bill of Rights, are considered a part of the original Constitution although they were not approved during the Constitutional Convention. The first Congress approved the Bill of Rights in 1789 and two years later the states completed the ratification process. The Constitution has been amended twenty seven times, including the first ten amendments. Two amendments, XVIII and XXI, deal with the same subject, prohibition. Article V deals with the amendatory process. There are two ways to amend the Constitution and each involves a two-stage process. (1) Congress may propose an amendment by a two-thirds vote in each house or (2) two-thirds of the state legislatures request Congress to convene a national convention to propose amendments. Congress has never used the second process because it would not control such a convention. After Congress approves a proposed amendment, states may ratify it in either of two ways: (1) three-fourths of the state legislatures must approve the amendment or (2) states convene special conventions to vote on the proposed amendment. Either method requires a majority vote to approve the amendment. The founding fathers purposely made the amendatory process difficult because they wanted to prevent the proposal of frivolous amendments. The president plays no constitutional role in the amendatory process but may express approval or disapproval for a particular amendment. States must usually approve amendments within a seven-year period but Congress has discretion in determining the time frame for approval. Members of Congress sometimes propose amendments they know have no chance of approval. They usually do this to please some constituents that may feel strongly about an issue. The brevity of the Constitution is one reason why policy makers do not support the need for amendments. The brevity of the Constitution permits changes to occur without the necessity of formal amendments.

AMERICAN EXCEPTIONALISM

American exceptionalism refers to that body of thought that claims America is exceptional compared to other nations. This idea can be traced back to John Winthrop's 1630 sermon portraying America as a "City Upon a Hill." His message was clear. The United States would be like no other nation. In the nineteenth century Alexis de Tocqueville wrote about American exceptionalism in a book that continues to be essential reading. The claim of exceptionalism has several roots. One is the fact that the thirteen colonies embraced republican ideals including a commitment to freedom and equality. In 1776, most Americans embraced the ideas embedded in the Declaration of Independence and this too was exceptional. At the time, these were revolutionary ideas not accepted by many other nations. Adding a Bill of Rights to the Constitution is an example of exceptionalism. Exceptionalism also has a religious component. Some Americans embraced the idea that God made America's destiny manifest. Many immigrants came to America in search of religious freedom. American exceptionalism has an empirical component. The fact is that the thirteen colonies that won independence went on to become a superpower with huge economic resources and worldwide influence. Then there is the fact that America welcomed immigrants from different parts of the world that came here to find freedom and prosperity. No other country has been so welcoming of so many immigrants. American officials often claim that American policy is to help others, promote democracy, and spread freedom. Critics of the idea of American exceptionalism point to the State Department's publication each year detailing human rights abuses of other countries. The publication conveys the idea the United States has the right to sit in judgment of other nations. Critics reject this presumption. When President Nixon went to China in 1972 to win its cooperation in containing the Soviet Union, he said nothing about China's massive abuse of human rights resulting in the deaths of millions of people. When the cold war ended, the United States again became critical of China's human rights violations. The concept of exceptionalism is controversial and critics believe the claim is hypocritical. They believe, similar to other nations, that national interest determines American policy. National interest and American exceptionalism are not necessarily contradictory. Although American exceptionalism has many critics, it continues to influence American political thought. One may embrace some elements of American exceptionalism while rejecting others.

AMERICAN POLITICAL CULTURE

Certain values, beliefs, and attitudes dominate America's political culture. Ever since the rebellion against George III in 1776, Americans have distrusted politicians. This is evident in the fact that most Americans have an unfavorable attitude towards Congress, most of the time. Dislike or distrust of politicians and politics is evident in the low voting turnout in many elections. Americans often support the "outsider," the anti-Washington establishment figure. Cultural differences may cause deep disagreements particularly if they involve moral values. Issues such as abortion, gay marriage, and capital punishment may cause deep fissures in the society. Cultures do change. Three issues that at one time caused deep divisions in American society but no longer do are divorce, gays serving in the military, and Catholics running for president. Certain terms are associated with American political culture such as individualism, change, competition, liberty, and equality. Most Americans value dissent including the right to disagree about the importance of specific political values. Americans like the idea of change. The call for change is often a campaign theme in presidential elections although candidates are not always clear about specific changes they would like to make. The appeal of change is present despite or because of the difficulty of definition and implementation. Political culture plays a role in determining presidential candidates. For example, neither of the two political parties has nominated a Jew or a female to run for president although there are no legal barriers to prevent this. American political culture makes it difficult for third parties to be successful. Americans, including independent voters, identify with either the Republican Party or the Democratic Party when it comes to casting a ballot.

AMICUS CURIAE

Amicus Curiae is a "friend of the court" brief. It is usually submitted to an appellate court by a group or an organization not directly involved in the litigation but has an interest in the final decision of a court. "Friends" may submit a brief in support of one of the parties involved in the litigation. It is unclear whether such briefs influence Supreme Court decisions.

ANTI-FEDERALISTS

After victory in the Revolutionary War, the former colonists established a government but disagreed about its powers. The colonists rebelled against the unjust rule of George III and many were determined to prevent creating a government that might produce the same abuses. When the Constitutional Convention convened in 1787, its purpose was to amend the Articles of Confederation, not to write a new constitution. Many delegates at the convention were concerned about events such as Shay's rebellion. They did not think amending the Articles would be sufficient to deal with the many crises confronting the government, including rebellions. They wanted to discard the Articles because the government was too weak to be effective. The Anti-Federalists disagreed. They wanted to correct the weaknesses of the Articles and thought they could do this by amending the Articles. Samuel Adams, George Mason, and Thomas Paine were among the leaders of the Anti-Federalist movement. When the Constitution was completed, the Anti-Federalists worked to defeat its ratification. They believed it granted too much power to the national government thus endangering the states. They also feared the office of the president could be transformed into a monarchy. Those opposed to ratifying the Constitution wrote a series of articles that scholars eventually put together under the title, Anti-Federalist Papers. The Anti-Federalists lost their argument but were correct in anticipating the growth of power at the national level.

BILL OF ATTAINDER

A bill of attainder is a legislative act punishing someone for allegedly engaging in illegal activities without benefit of a trial. During the colonial period, the British government used bills of attainder to punish colonists engaged in activities the government opposed. After the revolution, some states adopted laws to punish people because of their pro-British activities during the revolution. At the Constitutional Convention delegates decided to prohibit Bills of Attainder. Congress cannot impose penalties on individuals or organizations because if it did so it would be acting as a judicial body rather than a legislative body. That would violate the separation of powers doctrine as well as the constitutional prohibition on Bills of Attainder.

BILL OF RIGHTS

The Bill of Rights, the first ten amendments to the Constitution, was not a part of the original Constitution. Some states threatened to reject the Constitution because of its absence. One fear that emerged during the ratification debates was the prospect of the national government abusing its powers. Colonists rebelled against British rule because it threatened basic freedoms. Proponents of a Bill of Rights not only feared the specific grant of power to the national government in the proposed constitution but also the implied powers. The government could define its powers expansively by relying on specific clauses in the Constitution such as the "necessary and proper" clause in Article I of the Constitution. At the time of the Constitutional Convention, most states had a bill of rights to protect people at the state level. Critics believed it was more imperative to have the same protection at the national level. Some delegates such as Alexander Hamilton opposed including a Bill of Rights in the proposed constitution because they feared any rights not included might be excluded, ignored, or denied. Hamilton was not alone in his opposition but to ensure ratification, he changed his position, and agreed to add a Bill of Rights. He and other supporters of the Constitution wanted to avoid convening another convention to amend the Constitution for fear a second convention could undo the many compromises already achieved. The Continental Congress approved the Bill of Rights in 1789. The states completed the ratification process in December 1791, two years after the delegates completed the writing of the Constitution. When the Bill of Rights first passed, it limited the powers of the national government and was not applicable to the states. This limitation was eventually changed. After the Civil War, the government began the process of applying provisions of the Bill of Rights to the states.

BLOCK GRANTS

A block grant is money the federal government distributes to the states to deal with things such as education, health care, road building, and others. Block grants come with relatively few strings regulating how states dispense the funds. Block grants, compared to categorical grants, give states more flexibility in dealing with problems. Categorical grants limit flexibility because they are much more specific in controlling how funds are spent. Some members of Congress prefer categorical grants because it gives them more control over spending. It also enables individual members of Congress to take credit for funding specific projects back home that may help win reelection. How the national government dispenses funds to the states is an important aspect of federalism. The federal government uses various formulas for determining the funds each state receives. The size of the population often determines the amount of money received but Congress considers other factors such as the ability of the state to use the money effectively. All states are eligible for block grants regardless of the size of the population. Many states welcomed President Reagan's policy of combining categorical grants into block grants. This was a part of his program to revitalize the states rather than permitting the national government to dictate how states should spend funds. Critics claim the government sometimes dispenses funds to favor those states governed by the same political party that controls Congress.

BLUE DOG DEMOCRATS

Blue Dog Democrats are a group of fiscally conservative Democrats in the House of Representatives that emphasize fiscal responsibility and pay as you go programs. They generally oppose deficit spending and are often at odds with liberals in their party and their leaders in Congress. Blue Dog Democrats willingly work with fiscally conservative Republicans to control deficit spending and promote national security. They often support foreign policy measures and military appropriations to strengthen America's military capabilities. In the past, a few Blue Dog Democrats crossed over and formally joined the Republican Party because they thought the switch in parties would help ensure election victories. The number of Blue Dog Democrats in Congress varies but they usually have approximately fifty members. Some represent conservative congressional districts that often vote for Republican candidates. At times, both political parties may need the support of the Blue Dog Democrats to pass legislation or to prevent its passage. This may give them the opportunity to determine the success or failure of legislation in the House because they can align with either political party. They may not be able to dictate the outcome of legislative battles but they sometimes are able to win important concessions. The Blue Dog coalition is not monolithic. Members may agree on fiscal issues but disagree on economic and social policies. In the 2010 congressional elections, the Blue Dog Democrats lost half their seats. Some liberal Democrats believed the party lost seats in the Congress because of the Blue Dogs. Their attacks on liberal Democrats were similar to those made by the Republican Party.

BOLL WEEVIL DEMOCRATS

The Boll Weevil Democrats was a term used in mid-twentieth century to describe southern conservative Democrats who supported many of the economic and social programs of Presidents Roosevelt and Truman but opposed civil rights and any policies that threatened to end segregation in the South. Making certain that blacks could not vote helped keep them out of the political process and thus guaranteed the power of the white Democrats that dominated the political life of the South from the time of the Civil War until the civil rights movement of the 1960s. In 1948, some Boll Weevil Democrats split from the Democratic Party. They created the States Rights Democratic Party (also called the Dixiecrat Party) and nominated Strom Thurmond for president. He succeeded in winning the electoral votes of four southern states but was unable to prevent Harry Truman's victory. The Boll Weevils morphed into the group known as the Blue Dog Democrats. The term Boll Weevil is no longer used.

BUNDLER

A bundler is someone who can raise money from his or her network of friends and colleagues and contribute it to a political campaign. Bundlers are generally wealthy individuals. Presidents are grateful for support received and they often reward bundlers, at least in a symbolic way, for their efforts. The president may invite bundlers to attend a White House event, a state dinner, or a round of golf.

BUREAUCRACY

Bureaucracy is composed of those institutions and agencies that help make, interpret, and enforce laws, rules, and regulations. As the size of the government has increased so has the power of bureaucratic institutions. One source of power is the expertise of the bureaucrats who often remain in office for long periods. Bureaucrats are powerful because they often have discretion in determining whether laws will be implemented and how vigorously they will be implemented. They may also influence the legislative process in determining the final drafting of a bill. When Congress passed Title IX in 1972 to prevent gender discrimination, it did not define the meaning of equality because of its many ramifications. Bureaucrats were empowered to make that judgment on a case-by-case basis. Judicial decisions are not always definitive and are open to different interpretations. Once again, this gives bureaucrats a great deal of power and discretion. Presidents often complain that bureaucrats have too much power in determining how laws are passed and how they will be implemented. They may play a key role in supporting or opposing a president's legislative proposals. Bureaucrats play a major role at every stage of the legislative process. Conservatives are often critical of bureaucrats because of their power to write rules and regulations needed to implement legislation. If Congress passes a one thousand page bill, bureaucrats may then write thousands of pages of rules and regulations. Some critics believe these bureaucratic rules and regulations are often costly and enable bureaucrats to exercise too much power. Politicians must answer to the voters, bureaucrats do not. Bureaucrats, as they should be, are insulated from public opinion.

CATEGORICAL GRANTS

A categorical grant is money the national government dispenses to the states to deal with various problems. These grants impose conditions dealing with such things as the distribution of funds, their purpose, and what groups will receive the most benefits. States often have little discretion in dealing with categorical grants. They sometimes complain that meeting federal standards results in too much grant money going to bureaucracies to comply with various national requirements. What this means is that the national government may dictate how the states should spend money their citizens have sent to Washington. Some grants require states to come up with matching funds if they are to receive the grant. Without sufficient matching funds, states cannot compete. Categorical grants often require states or local governments to submit regular reports to Washington to make certain they comply with required standards. Governors prefer to receive block grants because they have fewer restrictions. Congress generally distributes grants, both categorical and block, on a formula or project basis. President Reagan favored block grants because, as a conservative, he wished to have states exercise more control over their resources and policies. He also believed states could demonstrate greater flexibility than Washington bureaucrats could.

CHURCH AND STATE: SEPARATION OF

The relationship between church and state in America has always been controversial. Many immigrants came to America in search of religious freedom. The ideal of American exceptionalism has always had a religious element dating all the way back to 1630 when John Wintrop delivered his City on the Hill sermon. The Supreme Court is often called upon to resolve church-state difficulties. There is no doubt that religion plays a more important role in America than in most other democracies. Thomas Jefferson once talked about a wall of separation between church and state but his comments were relevant to Great Britain, not the United States. In the United States there has never been a wall of separation between the two. A good example of how difficult it is to separate the two is the policy of some states to pay for text books used in religious schools. Proponents of such aid argue that providing the books promotes better education, not religious values. Proponents of separation oppose such policies.

CIVIL LAW

Civil law is a body of laws dealing with non-criminal issues such as contract disputes, property disputes, or divorce proceedings. Standards of guilt differ from criminal law. Individuals that lose a case are not subject to incarceration but there may be monetary penalties. People or companies or corporations found guilty of contract violations may have to pay punitive damages. The three main types of civil law deal with torts, contracts, and administrative law. Individuals can protect themselves from tort claims by purchasing insurance. Automobile insurance is an example of such protection as is medical malpractice insurance. Administrative law covers a wide range of activities engaged in by government agencies. It has become increasingly important due to the increased size and functions of the government.

CIVIL RIGHTS AND CIVIL LIBERTIES

Civil rights are rights given by the government and they may have a profound impact on how the political system functions. Civil rights include such things as who may vote and qualifications for voting. Women in America did not have the right to vote in national elections until the passage of Nineteenth Amendment in 1920. The minimum age for voting was twenty-one until passage of the Twenty Second Amendment in 1971. It lowered the minimum age to eighteen. Democratic governments determine such things as voting qualifications, eligibility for holding office, and curbs on religious practices. There may also be controversy regarding how the government protects basic rights and prevents abuses the government might inflict on unpopular minorities. Rights must be protected but how this is done can raise constitutional questions. Democratic political systems interpret civil rights differently based in part on cultural values. For example, there is no universal agreement on the best minimum age for being eligible to vote or holding public office. Civil liberties are liberties all individuals allegedly have because of the individual's basic worth. Governments do not confer civil liberties and therefore theoretically cannot deny them. Civil liberties are to be found in the Bill of Rights and include things such as freedom from arbitrary arrest, right to a fair trial, and freedom of religion. Many non-democratic governments do not recognize civil liberties and severely curtail civil rights. Such governments may permit elections but the government must approve those seeking office because they want to control the outcome.

CIVIL RIGHTS ACT 1964

The 1964 Civil Rights Act was one of a series of measures designed to prohibit discrimination and segregation in many areas of American life. The 1964 act is historically significant because its purpose was to extend basic rights to those long denied these rights because of discriminatory policies. President Kennedy first proposed the legislation in June 1963. After his assassination later in the month, President Johnson took up the cause and broadened the provisions of the proposed legislation. He was adept at manipulating the legislative process because of his many years as a congressional leader. Many southerners in Congress bitterly opposed President Johnson's civil rights proposals but he cleverly exploited the assassination of Kennedy to win broad public support for the legislation. It finally became law in 1964. The law had a profound impact on racial relations in the United States because of its broad sweep prohibiting discrimination. Among other things, it increased the number of Afro-Americans eligible to vote and thereby increased the number holding public office. The act outlawed discrimination in hiring practices enabling more Afro-Americans to compete in the job market. Subsequently, Title VII of the Civil Rights

Act guaranteed equal rights for women thereby making the extension of civil rights more universal and comprehensive. One consequence of the 1964 act was a political realignment in party identification. The Democratic Party controlled much of the South since the Civil War but after 1964 southern states began voting for Republican Party candidates. The realignment permanently ended the voting coalition President Roosevelt put together in 1932.

CIVIL SOCIETY

Civil society refers to the voluntary institutions people create or join to participate in the democratic process. Supporters of civil society argue that without these voluntary institutions, democracy may not have much meaning. They point to the fact that totalitarian systems sometimes permit elections but prohibit voluntary organization not controlled by the government from participating in the process. In a genuine civil society, these groups have the opportunity to debate and criticize government proposals and candidates running for office that support the government. There is no generally accepted definition of the term civil society and as a result, how governments define the term may be controversial. Although the term is often associated with democratic government, some analysts insist this is not necessarily the case. They point out that some organizations such as the Klu Klux Klan, the Mafia, terrorist organizations, white supremacists organizations, as well as those supporting fascism are voluntary organization that are decidedly undemocratic. During the cold war, the Soviet Union often organized "voluntary" groups to promote Soviet objectives. Groups associated with civil society have become increasingly important because of the information revolution but non-democratic governments can and do curtail their activities. The government may subject individuals in these groups to criminal penalties. The government may arrest or expel individuals from foreign countries promoting a cause the government opposes. Officials may intercept E-mails making it difficult or impossible for members of anti-government groups to communicate with each other. Nongovernmental organizations are associated with civil society but most of these organizations are not responsible to anyone but themselves. They may in fact support policies in a country opposed by a majority of the population.

CIVIL WAR AMENDMENTS

Policy makers often refer to the 13th, 14th, and 15th amendments as the civil war amendments. Supporters of the amendments intended to bring about the reconstruction of the southern states. Northern leaders believed that reconstruction was necessary to help justify the costs of the war. The 13th Amendment abolished slavery. The 15th Amendments gave former slaves the right to vote but the southern states erected many barriers that effectively prevented blacks from voting. The 14th Amendment is the most sweeping of the three. It guaranteed citizenship to all people born or naturalized in the United States. It also contains the "equal protection" clause and the "due process" clause. Advocates of the equal protection clause wanted to make certain states did not violate rights guaranteed in the Constitution. The due process clause prohibits states the power to deny people their "life, liberty, or property without due process of law." Eventually, the Supreme Court interpreted the 14th Amendment to make most parts of the Bill of Rights applicable to the states. After the 1932 presidential election, the Supreme Court issued rulings that greatly expanded the powers of the national government at the expense of the states.

CLOTURE

Members of the Senate have the right to engage in extended debates called filibusters. A minority number of Senators opposed to a bill may debate it indefinitely unless Senators agree to invoke cloture, a process for ending debate in the Senate. In the past, southern Senators used the filibuster to prevent passage of civil rights legislation. Before the 1964 Civil Rights Act, blacks in southern states did not have the right to vote. Southern Senators used the filibuster to preserve the status quo and retain their power. In 1975, the Senate curbed the right to filibuster by changing the rules of debate. Sixteen Senators must approve a motion to invoke cloture. Three-fifths of the Senate, sixty votes, must vote affirmatively to approve cloture and thereby end debate. In the past, a two-thirds vote of the entire Senate was necessary to end a filibuster. Those supporting cloture do so because they believe the majority should have the opportunity to cast a ballot on pending legislation after debates have gone on for a reasonable period of time. Those supporting filibusters claim the procedure helps protect minority opinions. Allegedly, extended debate serves an educational purpose but that claim never had much validity.

COATTAIL EFFECT

The coattail effect occurs when an individual wins an election because of his or her association with a popular leader who has the support of the American people. The coattail effect is generally associated with presidential elections. An example of this is when a voter casts a ballot for a popular presidential candidate and other members of his political party. When voters elected Franklin Roosevelt in 1932, his popularity enabled many Democrats to defeat their Republican opponents in congressional races. Democrats controlled

Congress the entire time he was in power. They retained control of Congress until 1952. The coattail factor is less significant now than in the past. Many American voters now split their ballot electing a Republican or a Democrat for president and members of the other party for Congress. Another factor is that individuals running for Congress now get much more media exposure than in the past enabling voters to be more discriminating because they know much more about congressional candidates than they did in the past. Analysts sometimes have difficulty accurately gauging the coattail effect of a popular candidate. Barak Obama won the 2008 presidential election winning three hundred sixty-five electoral votes to one hundred seventy three for his opponent, John McCain. Obama was obviously a popular candidate. That year Democrats also won control of both houses of Congress. Although their victory was in part attributable to Obama's popularity, the vote was also an anti-Republican Party vote. Experts assume that many Democrats won congressional seats that year because of the anti-Bush sentiment that was already evident in the 2006 congressional elections. The Democrats won control of both houses of Congress two years before the Obama victory. They simply enlarged their majorities in 2008.

COMMANDER IN CHIEF

Article II of the Constitution spells out the powers of the president including his power as Commander in Chief. As with many other parts of the Constitution, Article II is subject to different interpretations. As the commander of the armed forces, the president often decides, without a declaration of war, to dispatch America's armed forces abroad. He may do so for a variety of reasons including assassination of target individuals, to gather information, to rescue hostages, peacekeeping missions, or to gather information. Since 1945, the United States fought four major wars, Korea, Vietnam, Iraq, and

Afghanistan without Congress formally declaring war. This precedent dates back to President Jefferson. He used the president's war powers to initiate defensive measures to protect vessels threatened by pirates off the Barbary Coast. He initiated this action without first seeking congressional approval although eventually he did so. The president may send troops abroad on a rescue mission or for humanitarian reasons without consulting Congress. The Commander in Chief clause has become very contentious because presidents tend to interpret it very broadly. They have relied on war powers to justify certain domestic policies related to foreign threats that allegedly affect America's national security. President George W. Bush relied on the war powers in developing policies related to national security issues after the terrorist attack on 9/11. He characterized the attack as an act of war and then initiated a number of controversial policies some critics claimed were unconstitutional. Often there are no clear demarcation lines between legal and illegal or constitutional and unconstitutional. America's role in the world helps define the president's power as Commander In Chief.

COMMERCE CLAUSE

The commerce clause in Article I, section 8, of the Constitution simply states that Congress has the right "to regulate commerce with foreign Nations and among the States . . . ." The clause has brought about a huge growth in the power of the national government because officials often combined the commerce clause with the "necessary and proper clause." This combination has enabled the government to regulate many things only remotely related to commerce such as child labor, racial segregation, monitoring food and drug safety, and certain types of advertising. Strict constructionists believe the clause has been more broadly defined than the founding fathers intended. Since the adoption of the Constitution, interstate and global commerce have become increasingly important resulting in more government regulations. Much of the expansion of the government's power is associated with Supreme Court decisions that have broadly interpreted the meaning of the commerce clause. The court has ruled that commerce includes commercial activity. Congress can use this phrase to include many things Congress wants to regulate. Congress and the courts can interpret the term commercial activity in many different ways. Power has also drifted towards the national government because it can print money and assume debts. Some states, unlike the national government, are legally required to balance their budget.

COMMON SENSE

Common Sense, written by Thomas Paine played an important role in winning support for the rebellion against George III. His pamphlet sold more than 150,000 copies. Paine had the ability to write in a style that appealed to the common man. He was particularly effective in attacking monarchical rule. He claimed it was obsolete and unjust.

CONCURRENT POWERS

The American Constitution distributes power between national and state governments in three ways delegated, reserved, and concurrent. Concurrent powers are those shared by the national and state governments. Examples of concurrent powers include taxation, creating courts, and borrowing money. Demarcation lines separating the three distributions are not always easy to discern. Changing conditions are an important factor. Some powers, such as those dealing with education, were once considered reserved powers but are now more appropriately labeled concurrent powers. On some issues such as speeding laws, the national government may temporarily take control although controlling speed limits is a reserved power. The national government does this by threatening to withhold funds from the states if they do not "voluntarily" comply with regulations promulgated by a national agency or department. During an emergency, the national government will sometimes usurp state powers.

CONCURRENT RESOLUTION

The House of Representatives and the Senate must approve concurrent resolutions but they do not have the force of law nor does Congress send them to the president for his signature. Congress may pass a resolution to congratulate a sports team for a victory or to express sorrow for a tragedy such as a tsunami or an earthquake. Concurrent resolutions may establish budgetary goals for the next fiscal year. Congress may approve a concurrent resolution to amend rules applicable to both houses of Congress or to establish a joint committee. Concurrent resolutions and joint resolutions are distinct and should not be confused. The latter have the force of law similar to bills passed by Congress.

CONFEDERATION

After winning independence, the United States created a confederation composed of the thirteen states and the national government. The American confederation limited the powers of the national government and granted sovereignty to each of the thirteen states. The outstanding characteristic of the American confederation was the inability of the national government to deal directly with people. For example, in a confederation, if the national government needs funds it cannot go directly to the people and impose a tax. The national government must rely on state governments to raise revenues but states do not always do what the national government would like them to do. While the Articles of Confederation were in effect, the government had difficulty dealing with the many problems that arose after winning independence because they often required the cooperation of the states that was not always forthcoming. In 1789, delegates at the Constitutional Convention discarded the confederation and adopted a federal form of government. Today, a number of countries have a confederal form of government. The distribution of power in a confederation varies from one nation to another.

CONFERENCE COMMITTEE

A congressional conference committee is a temporary committee composed of members from both houses of Congress, the House and Senate. Its purpose is to reconcile differences in legislation passed by the two houses. Congress cannot send a bill to the president for his signature unless both houses have passed legislation using the same language. The conference committee is composed of individuals from both houses that served on the committees that originally passed the legislation. The reconciliation process can be contentious if one political party does not control both houses of Congress. When a conference committee reconciles differences, a majority of each party, Republicans and Democrats, must approve the changes. The committee cannot combine the yes votes of both political parties to achieve a majority. Once the conference committee reconciles the differences, the legislation then goes back to the House and Senate for a final vote. Neither house can make any changes in the legislation produced by the conference committee. Once the House and Senate approve the amended version of the bill, the legislation then goes to the president for his approval or veto. After reconciling House and Senate differences, the conference committee disbands.

CONGRESSIONAL BUDGET OFFICE

Congress created the Congressional Budget Office (CBO) in 1974. Its function is to advise Congress on budgetary matters. It plays a major role in the budgetary process by estimating government revenue, estimating the costs of programs, and financing the national debt. The office is nonpartisan. If a congressional committee wants to know the cost of a proposed program, the Congressional Office will only use the figures supplied by the committee to determine the final cost. The CBO cannot use its own figures or estimates. As a result, the quality of some CBO reports is only as good as the information they have to work with. The CBO does evaluate the president's budget and this enables members of Congress to make more informed judgments regarding the president's proposals. The CBO also makes judgments about the cost of entitlement programs due to changing circumstances. If there is an increase in the number of people eligible to receive social security benefits, the CBO will estimates the costs. The CBO also studies long term budgetary trends such as future costs of entitlement programs. The national budget, because it involves such huge sums of money, is a complicated document that impacts much of American life. Many policy makers are unfamiliar with the entire budget because they are primarily concerned about those portions of the budget related to their policy concerns. The CBO is one of the few agencies that examine the budget in its entirety.

CONGRESSIONAL CAUCUSES

There are congressional caucuses that represent ethnic or religious groups, economic interests, regional issues, and many others. There are caucus groups for every imaginable issue. Such groups include Congressional Boating Caucus, Congressional Caucus on Hellenic Issues, the Sex and Violence in the Media Caucus, and the Unexploded Ordinance Caucus. The latter promotes efforts to eliminate unexploded ordinances that kill and maim many people each year. Some of these devices date back to World War II. A caucus may have members from one or both houses of Congress. The power of a caucus depends on such things as the party in power, membership size, unity, and prestige. A caucus sometimes behaves in much the same way as an interest group. Caucus members try to convince non-members to support or oppose specific legislation. The number of caucuses varies as members create new ones and old ones disappear. Congress officially recognizes more than one hundred caucuses.

CONGRESSIONAL POLITICAL PARTY CAUCUSES

In Congress, both the Democratic and Republican parties have a party caucus in each house of Congress. Each caucus basically has the same functions. A caucus is simply a closed meeting of a political party to decide or debate one or more political issues. The party caucus is composed of all members of the party serving in either the House or Senate. These meetings help determine party policies and strategies. They give members an opportunity to express their ideas on policy options and to propose issues for future consideration. The caucus nominates and elects party leaders, approves committee assignments, enforces rules, makes committee assignments, and helps members win reelection. A major purpose of the party caucus is to promote party unity. Winning candidates from the same political party may have divergent interests. The party caucus is a major instrument for developing a unified front. If the caucus is unable to reconcile differences it may at least devise strategies that minimize them.

CONNECTICUT PLAN

At the 1787 Constitutional Convention, differences between the large and small states regarding representation in the proposed national legislature threatened the hoped for success at the convention. The representation issue was difficult and contentious because it dealt with the distribution of power at several different levels. The Virginia Plan for representation would have enabled the largest states to control the legislative process at the national level. The New Jersey Plan favored the smaller states. The plan basically kept intact the structure of the national legislature as it was under the Articles of Confederation. The Connecticut Plan, also known as the Great Compromise, combined portions of each thus resolving a major issue at the Constitutional Convention. The Great Compromise created a bicameral legislature. Population would determine representation in the House of Representatives but each state would have equal representation in the Senate. The slave states wanted one chamber to represent their states as a means to protect slavery. Reconciling the interests of the large and small states was a major accomplishment at the Constitutional Convention and contributed to the success of the convention and the approval of the Constitution.

CONSERVATISM

Conservatism has a number of core beliefs including limited government, protection of fundamental freedoms, fiscal responsibility, and support for traditions. Conservatives support a strong national defense and give national security issues a high priority. Most conservatives support limited government and free market economic systems. Despite the core beliefs, conservative thought in America is not monolithic. Conservatives may advocate and support fundamentally different foreign policies. Some conservatives support a muscular foreign policy to help shape the international environment to better reflect American values. In 2003, President H. Bush decided to invade Iraq. One of his expectations was that a victory there would help transform the region by promoting democratic values. Few people anticipated the length of the conflict or its costs, human and material. Other conservatives prefer a more modest role for the United States in world affairs to better control military spending and avoid unnecessary foreign entanglements. They want a narrow definition of America's national interests and are always aware of the law of unintended consequences. Conservatives often disagree about the government's role in regulating social behavior but they agree that major changes in a political system should come slowly. They generally oppose policies such as affirmative action because they believe such policies tend to be unjustly discriminatory. They also oppose broad legislative proposals that seek to do for people what they can do for themselves. It is incorrect to assume conservatives oppose change; they generally oppose fundamental change that significantly alters the status quo. They prefer incremental change.

CONSTITUENCY

A constituency is the group of people represented by an elected official. A narrower definition would be to only include individuals that voted for the incumbent. Senators represent a larger constituency than do members of the House and therefore represent more diversified interests. Senators from large states such as California or New York must deal with many issues including agricultural, manufacturing, ethnic and racial. Larger states may also have significant foreign policy interests they wish to protect. Such interests would include trade, travel, military missions, and diplomatic activity. American foreign policy vis-à-vis Cuba after

1959 was to a considerable extent influenced by Cuban exiles living in Miami that fled to America after Castro came to power in 1959. A candidate's policy recommendations for dealing with Castro may determine how the voter casts his ballot. Congress has often sided with Greece in its difficulties with Turkey because there are more Greek voters in America than Turkish voters. Greek voters use their power to influence foreign policy. Minority groups will sometimes cast their ballot in congressional or presidential races based on a single interest important to the group. Members of Congress are always sensitive to demographic changes in their state or district that may influence voting behavior. They have a much easier time satisfying the needs of people back home if their interests are homogeneous. If legislators represent districts or states characterized by groups with conflicting interests, the legislator will try to achieve a balance between and among the groups. Small constituency groups with strong feelings may be more important than large groups with more diverse interests.

CONTINENTAL CONGRESS

The first Continental Congress convened in 1774. Members of the Congress wanted George III to treat the colonies more fairly but he was more concerned about protecting his authority. He was unsympathetic to the many complaints of the colonists and was determined to have his rule respected. He was an absolute ruler who demanded absolute obedience from his subjects. At the time, monarchs expected obedience. A second Continental Congress convened 1775. It created the Continental Army and appointed George Washington as its leader. The Congress issued the Declaration of Independence in July 1776 that severed the relationship between the colonies and the mother country. It then had the responsibility to lead the new nation in the struggle for independence.

COURT PACKING PLAN

In 1937, President Roosevelt introduced a plan to increase the number of judges serving on the Supreme Court. He was angry because the court invalidated, usually by five to four votes, some important New Deal policies put into effect after his election in 1932. His policies were intended to cope with the consequences of the 1929 economic depression. F.D.R. wanted to increase the number of judges that would make certain the approval of his New Deal legislation. The Senate rejected Roosevelt's proposal because it violated the principles associated with the separation of powers doctrine. The Senate rejected Roosevelt's court reform legislation despite his overwhelming reelection in 1936. He won forty six states of forty eight states. Roosevelt discarded his proposed changes to the court in 1937 when one of the judges switched his vote. The court then began to approve New Deal legislation previously rejected. This led one critic to quip, "a switch in time saved nine." Members of the court are always aware of public opinion but it is difficult to know how it influences individual court decisions. Roosevelt was president long enough to enable him to place eight of his nominees on the bench. The eight judges influenced decisions long after Roosevelt's death in 1945.

CRITICAL ELECTION

A critical election, sometimes referred to as a realigning election, occurs when a majority of voters change their party allegiance because of a major event, changes in the composition of the population, or dissatisfaction with the majority party. The realignment enables the victorious party to retain control of the government for an extended period. The last critical election was 1932 when a majority of voters began to support the Democratic Party. Voters elected President

Roosevelt four times: 1932, 1936, 1940, 1944. Harry Truman, a democrat won the 1948 election. Before 1932, most voters supported the Republican Party. It won the presidential contests in 1920, 1924, and 1928. Republicans controlled Congress from 1918 to 1932. Since World War II, realignment occurs more slowly. Secular realignment is the slow shift in party identification. Both terms, secular and critical, are now less significant than in the past. Voters now are more likely to split their ballot between the parties. There is also the fact that fewer people identify with either the Republican or the Democratic parties on more than a temporary basis. Many voters like to think of themselves as independent although they continue to vote for either of the two major parties. Split ticket voting now seems to be the norm. More voters now identify themselves as independent and will cast ballots for the candidate they think best serves their interests regardless of party affiliation.

DARK HORSE CANDIDATES

A dark horse candidate refers to someone who must overcome major obstacles to win a nomination or an election. There is almost always a dark horse candidate trying to win in the presidential primaries. The dark horse candidate must usually overcome the problem of name recognition and inadequate funding. Dark horse candidate candidates sometimes succeed in overcoming the problem of name recognition and go on to win the nomination, but most fail. Some who succeeded includes Jimmy Carter who became the Democratic Party's presidential nominee in 1976. Bill Clinton was a dark horse candidate for his party's nomination in 1992. He not only won the nomination contest but he unexpectedly went on to defeat President George H. W. Bush who was seeking a second term. Barak Obama was a dark horse entering the Democratic Party primaries in the 2008 presidential election but once nominated he lost the dark horse label.

In the presidential race, he easily defeated his Republican rival, John McCain.

DE FACTO SEGREGATION

There are two types of de facto segregation. One type is the result of patterns or habits but is not legally mandated. Throughout America there are neighborhoods populated by a particular ethnic or racial group. People that are not a part of that group may not want to live in such neighborhoods simply because they do not share the same values as the majority. People are often more comfortable living in neighborhoods where they are a part of the majority. There is also a de facto segregation designed to keep specific groups of people out of certain neighborhoods because of prejudice. Home owners and real estate agents may purposely refuse to sell real estate to certain groups.

DELEGATED POWERS

The Constitution distributes power between national and state governments in three ways: delegated, reserved, and concurrent. Delegated powers are those assigned to the national government such as the regulation of interstate commerce, coining money, and declaring war. Article 1, section 8, of the Constitution lists the delegated powers but the Article can be misleading because it lists only eighteen powers thus giving the impression of limited powers. Article I, section 8, also contains the "necessary and proper clause" that Congress has relied on to substantially increase the powers of the national government beyond the eighteen powers specifically listed. The commerce clause in Article I also helped expand the powers of the national government. As the economy morphed from agriculture to industry and then became more service oriented, the government relied on the commerce clause to regulate the economy and other aspects of American life. This trend became more pronounced as trade became more national and then more global. Parts of the 1964 Civil Rights Act is based on the commerce clause that now also includes commercial activity.

DEMOCRATIC PARTY

The Democratic Party is America's oldest political party dating back to Thomas Jefferson. Some of the most important presidents elected on the Democratic Party ticket include Andrew Jackson, Woodrow Wilson, Franklin Roosevelt, Harry Truman, and Lyndon Johnson. President Roosevelt and the Democratic Party played a major role in dealing with the 1929 economic crash and World War II. President Truman presided over the transition from a war time to a peacetime economy after 1945 and put into place the foundation for the cold war policies dealing with the Soviet Union. Lyndon Johnson extended the social and economic policies of the New Deal under the leadership of President Roosevelt. The Democratic Party believes the government should play a major role in shaping economic and social programs to improve the quality of life. The Democratic Party usually articulates its principles in a sufficiently general way to permit broad interpretations. This enables both the liberal and conservative wings of the party to unite during the electoral process for the sake of party unity and defeating the opposition. Although distinctions between the two parties are often blurred, the fact is they fundamentally differ on many issues. Observers determine this by studying how members of each party vote in Congress. On major issues there is almost always a clear demarcation line between Republicans and Democrats.

DEVOLUTION

Devolution is the process whereby a central government will grant powers to subunits such as regions or states or local units. The national government may approve a program but leave its implementation to the smaller units of government. Those that support devolution argue that the national government either has too much power or is not flexible enough to deal with problems that may have many variations from region to region or state to state. Devolution may also occur at the state level. A state government may create and disband local units of government for different projects. A good example of devolution is the degree of autonomy enjoyed by the District of Columbia. It may approve laws and regulations but Congress can nullify them if it disapproves of these policies.

DISCHARGE PETITION

A discharge petition is now a rarely used procedure by which a majority in the House of Representatives would sign a petition to force a bill out of a committee despite the opposition of the chair. In the past, some members of Congress tried to use this procedure when southerners were committee chairs and would refuse to hold hearings on a bill particularly if the subject was civil rights. Committee chairs no longer have the power they once did and as a result, the discharge petition is now rarely used.

DISCRETIONARY SPENDING

Discretionary spending is money appropriated by Congress on an annual basis that is not legally mandated for things such as social security or Medicare. Most government expenditures results from legally mandated programs. Discretionary spending amounts to about forty percent of the total budget. Members of Congress will sometimes use discretionary spending for pet projects that will help them win reelection but they also appropriate money to deal with issues that contribute to the welfare of the American people. Defense expenditures are an example of discretionary spending.

DIVIDED GOVERNMENT

Divided government occurs when different political parties control the executive and legislative branches of government. It also occurs when different political parties control the House and Senate. Divided government may produce one of two results: either deadlock or compromise. If the two parties are primarily interested in promoting ideological goals, they will find it difficult to cooperate with each other. If moderates dominate the two parties, they will find compromises acceptable to both. Whether divided government is good or not is a value judgment. Over the years, the number of independent voters has increased and they often split their ticket by voting for Republicans and Democrats. Legislative deadlock may result if members of the two parties are unable to reconcile their differences because of ideology. Ideological differences are often based on differences about important principles, not just policy differences. Divided government makes it difficult for voters to determine what party is responsible for legislative deadlock. The problem of assigning responsibility for success or failure in policy making is also complicated by the fact that American political parties are not as disciplined as parties in parliamentary political systems. Office holders in either the Democratic or Republican parties will often disagree with their leaders and vote against their proposed programs.

DIXIECRATS

In 1948, a group of southern Democrats unhappy with the provisions in the Democratic Party platform dealing with civil rights, bolted the party and organized the Democratic States Rights Party, often called the Dixiecrat Party. It carried four states in the presidential election but failed to prevent President Truman's victory. **After his election, the Dixiecrat Party faded away but** southerners supporting segregation remained in power in the South until the civil rights movement in the 1960s. The 1964 Civil Rights Act and a number of Supreme Court decisions substantially reduced the power of southern Democrats. The Republican Party became much more popular in the South and won many congressional seats formerly controlled by Democrats. Third parties usually do not have a long life span and third party candidates rarely win elections. Third parties exist because of voter dissatisfaction with the two major parties, the Republicans and Democrats.

DON'T ASK, DON'T TELL

After Bill Clinton's election as president in 1988, gay rights groups wanted him to eliminate the ban on homosexuals serving in the armed forces. Gay rights activists claimed the government was violating the civil rights of homosexuals by not permitting them to serve. The gay rights movement was part of the civil rights movement demanding an end to discriminatory practices. Some military leaders opposed the proposed changes because they feared the impact on morale. President Clinton persuaded Congress to adopt a Don't Ask, Don't Tell policy. Homosexuals could serve in the armed forces provided they did not make their sexual orientation known. Officers could not question personnel about their sexual orientation unless they had a specific reason for doing so. Although gay rights groups were pleased with the change, they did not think it went far enough. They claimed the Clinton policy was also discriminatory. After his election in 2008, Barak Obama ended the "don't ask, don't tell" policy. He opposed separate standards that discriminated against gays. They could now openly serve in the military without concealing their sexual preferences.

DUE PROCESS

There is a due process clause in the fifth and fourteenth amendments to the Constitution. Due process has two elements, substantive and procedural. Substantive due process deals with basic rights. After the civil war the Supreme Court incorporated most rights in the Bill of Rights into the Fourteenth Amendment and made them applicable to the states. This is the incorporation doctrine. Before the civil war, the Bill of Rights applied only to the national government. Substantive due process acts as a check on the government to prevent its abuse of power. The courts might review any government policies that seek to curb basic freedoms or basic rights if they think such policies violate substantive due process clause of the Fourteenth Amendment. Procedural due process guarantees the government will not unfairly deprive an individual of life, liberty, or property. If, for example, the government charges an individual with a crime, the charge must have legitimate supporting evidence. If the government puts an individual on trial, the judge must be fair and the jury impartial. These are essential elements for a fair trial. If a convicted individual thinks he has not received a fair trial because of the actions of the judge or jury, he may appeal the verdict. There is a "due process" clause in both the fifth and fourteenth amendments to the Constitution that helps guarantee such things as a fair trial, the equal protection of the law, and protection against unjust discrimination based on gender, race, or religion. Procedural due process is concerned with how things get done. An example would be procedures followed in a criminal case. How a judge rules and the selection of juries are examples of due process. In a criminal case lawyers carefully review the process leading to a verdict.

EARMARKS

An earmark is the practice that permits members of Congress to insert additions to legislative bills that direct money to a particular project favorable to the member and the district or state he or she represents. An earmark may take up just a few lines in a bill that may be hundreds of pages long. Critics dislike earmarks because they add billions of dollars to the budget. Members of Congress, including sponsors of legislation, are often unaware that colleagues have inserted earmarks in the legislation. Some members consider this an advantage because the earmark receives less scrutiny during the legislative process but they make certain the voters back home know who is responsible for benefits received. Most members of Congress like earmarks because it enables them to boast about what they have done for their constituency and this often helps members win reelection. Congressmen believe they are more competent to determine how to allocate money earmarked for their district or state than nameless bureaucrats in Washington. The use of earmarks has increased over the years and so has criticism of the practice. Legislators often insert the earmarks during the process of reconciling legislation passed by the House and Senate. When the conference committee agrees on a bill, it goes back to each house for a vote. Neither house can amend the legislation. It must be accepted or rejected but not amended. Critics sometimes use the terms, earmarks and pork, interchangeable although there are important differences between the two.

ELASTIC CLAUSE

The elastic clause, also known as the necessary and proper clause, is located in Article I, section 8, of the Constitution. The elastic clause enables the government to be flexible in dealing with new problems but it has also contributed to the expansion of the national government's power because it can determine what is necessary and what is proper. There is no objective definition of what is necessary and proper. Delegates at the 1787 Constitutional Convention vigorously debated the clause. Opponents feared that a broad interpretation of the clause would greatly expand the power of the national government and this in fact has happened. The elastic clause was one reason why the anti-Federalists opposed ratifying the Constitution. They were correct in anticipating the consequences of adopting the clause. The Anti-Federalists opposed other parts of the Constitution as well. Even without the elastic clause, they probably would have voted against ratifying the Constitution.

ELECTION 1800

Although most of the Founding Fathers opposed political, they came about somewhat spontaneously because of differences between the Democratic Republicans and the Federalists. Critics consider the 1800 presidential election as the birth of the party system in America. By that time, differences between the followers of Hamilton and Jefferson were evident. The two sides differed on the creation of a national bank and they supported different sides in the war between France and Great Britain. Thomas Jefferson was the leader of the Democratic Republicans. Many observers considered Hamilton the leader of the Federalists but in 1800 John Adams was president and was seeking a second term. The Federalists controlled the national government since the ratification of the Constitution in 1789. By the time of the 1800 presidential election, the Federalists had become unpopular and internally divided. Jefferson won the 1800 election.

ELECTORAL COLLEGE

Presidential election outcomes are determined by winning a majority of electoral votes in the Electoral College, not a majority of the popular vote. The winning candidate must win a minimum of 270 votes. In the past, four presidential candidates won the majority popular vote but failed to become president because they did not receive the requisite electoral votes. This happened in 1824, 1876, 1888, and 2000. The Electoral College is in keeping with America's federal system of government. Each state has a number of electoral votes determined by the size of the congressional delegation including members of the House and Senate. All but two states have a winner take all system. If a candidate wins the most popular votes, even if it is not an absolute majority, he receives all the electoral votes. Some critics dislike the winner take all provision because just a few votes may separate the two leading candidates but the winner gets all the electoral votes. Critics think the electoral votes awarded to a candidate should be proportional to the popular vote. Supporters of the two party system support the winner takes all system because it prevents third parties from fracturing the electoral system. The winner takes all system discourages third party candidates. Although third party candidates cannot win they can influence the outcome. In the 2000 presidential race, Al Gore lost the election because he lost Florida. Bush won the state in part because Ralph Nader, a third party candidate, took enough votes away from Gore to enable Bush to win Florida and the presidency. Every vote for a third party candidate is a vote one of the two major candidates does not receive. A candidate can win the presidency by winning in just eleven states with the most electoral votes but winning in all eleven states is unlikely. Presidential candidates spend most of their time campaigning in the large states with the most electoral votes. Some critics would like to abolish the Electoral College but every four years it produces a winner who generally supports retaining the system. Those who wrote the Constitution wanted an electoral college in part because they feared popular rule. When the delegates at the Constitutional Convention adopted the Constitution, electors in the Electoral College were public servants and did not reflect public opinion.

ELECTORAL COLLEGE DEADLOCK

Should no presidential candidate win a majority of votes in the Electoral College, the House of Representatives then determines the winning candidate. Each state delegation has one vote and they must cast it for any of the top three candidates as determined by the ranking of electoral votes they received in the presidential election. State delegations may not split their vote. The winner of the House vote need receive only a majority vote to become president. The House picked the winner in two presidential elections: 1800 and 1824. The Senate by majority vote determines who shall be Vice President. Unlike the House, the vote of each Senator is counted individually. Each senator from a state may vote for a different candidate even if both are members of the same political party. The possibility of an Electoral College deadlock is one reason why some critics would like to eliminate or reform the present system. It is possible to have a situation whereby one branch of Congress votes for a Democrat to become president while the other branch selects a Republican to become Vice President. The public usually does not have a high regard for Congress. Anyone that became president as a result of a congressional vote would probably not have much legitimacy. Fortunately, this situation is unlikely to come about.

ELECTORAL MANDATE

Winning presidential candidates often claim to have an electoral mandate but the claim can be difficult to prove because people cast their ballots for many different reasons. Occasionally, winning candidates may legitimately claim to have a mandate. In 1932, voters obviously wanted Roosevelt to do whatever was necessary to help the economy recover from the 1929 economic crash. In 1952, many voters cast their ballots for Eisenhower because of his promise to end the Korean War. In 1968, Richard Nixon's promise to end the Vietnam War won him much support. The war had become a very divisive issue in American politics. In both elections, in addition to the unpopularity of the wars, voters were generally dissatisfied with the party in power and sought a change. Although Barak Obama won the 2008 presidential race easily, there is no evidence he received a specific mandate. Many individuals that voted for Obama would have voted against any Republican. President H. Bush was very unpopular when he left office. In some polls, his approval rating was only nineteen percent. Voters simply wanted a change but such a demand may have many different and contradictory meanings. After Obama's election, many left wing voters who supported him claimed that several of his major policies, particularly in the area of foreign affairs and constitutional rights, were not much different from those of former President H. Bush. They did not get the changes they anticipated. Almost all newly elected presidents are surprised at how difficult it is to bring about major changes. In the American political system, it is easier to prevent change than to cause it because the system has many veto points that can effectively prevent or minimize changes. There are always interests supporting and protecting the status quo.

EMANCIPATION PROCLAMATION

President Lincoln issued two emancipation proclamations. In 1862, he issued the first proclamation freeing slaves in the Confederate states. He issued the second proclamation in 1863. It freed slaves in ten additional states. Opponents of the proclamations feared they would prolong the war because southern states were committed to the slave system and therefore would continue to fight as long as possible. Many historians consider the proclamations a major achievement of President Lincoln and a major event in American history. The proclamations and the outcome of the civil war ended slavery in America but racial problems continued. After the Civil War, the southern states gradually put into place policies that guaranteed racial segregation and continued discrimination. These polices remained in place until the 1960s. The Emancipation Proclamations helped keep voters in the southern states committed to the Democratic Party until 1964. After that date the Republican Party became much more competitive in the South.

EMPIRICAL

Empirical evidence is associated with facts—something may be factually correct or incorrect. It would be empirically correct to say that Barak Obama won the 2008 presidential election but it would be difficult to prove he won because of one particular factor. Two groups of people may have voted for him for contradictory reasons. Empirical is sometimes confused with causation or correlation. Two items or events may be empirically related without any reference to causation. A farmer from southern Illinois may vote for a Republican presidential candidate but that does not mean he did so because he farms or lives in southern Illinois. A majority of people in the same ethnic group may vote for a presidential candidate without ethnicity being a factor. Critics usually differentiate empirical from normative. People may like or dislike a president without being able to cite empirical evidence to support their argument. Normative judgments, such as liking or disliking a president, are value based but such judgments may also have supporting empirical evidence. There may be empirical evidence supporting the idea that a particular medical remedy is effective and therefore doctors value it because of that reason.

ENTITLEMENT PROGRAMS

Entitlement programs are those that people are entitled to simply because they meet some minimum standards applicable to a particular group. Examples are Social Security and health insurance programs such as Medicare. These programs are a major part of the federal budget and have a great deal of political support from beneficiaries of these programs. Once entitlement programs are in place, it is very difficult to reduce or eliminate benefits. Entitlement programs are a major factor in the swelling U.S. budget deficits at both the national and state levels. More than fifty percent of the national budget, the figure is a rough estimate, is committed to entitlement programs. Only Congress can reduce benefits but they are reluctant to do so because voters are likely to retaliate. Interest groups are vigilant in protecting the benefits of people they represent. One reason why entitlement programs are so expensive is that they often benefit a growing segment of the population. The aging American population has drastically increased the costs of the Social Security and Medicaid programs. After the election of Barak Obama in 2008, it became apparent the government would have to do something to better control the costs of the entitlement programs but there was no consensus in Congress about how they should do this. The lack of consensus resulted in substantial increases in the national debt.

ENUMERATED POWERS

Enumerated powers are located in Article I and other parts of the Constitution. Congress is not limited to the enumerated powers in the Constitution. Article 1 section 8, contains the "necessary and proper clause" that gives Congress the power to do what is necessary and proper to carry out its duties. Over the years, this section, because of its general nature, greatly expanded the power of Congress and the national government beyond the original enumerated powers. The necessary and proper clause was one reason why Anti-Federalists opposed ratifying the Constitution. They correctly anticipated the growing power of the national government. Article I also specifically grants Congress the power to regulate interstate commerce and this too has been a significant source of power as the American economy transitioned from agriculture to an industrial base and then to a post—industrial or service economy. The government needed new powers and regulations to cope with the changes. It is, for example, one thing for farmers to raise, kill, and sell chickens in their state. When this process involves more than one state, then the national government intervenes to help ensure the entire process conforms to national standards to protect such things as health and safety. Government regulations have also increased as a result of the growth of international trade. The enumerated powers are powers given to the national government, not the states.

ESTABLISHMENT CLAUSE

The First Amendment to the Constitution states, "Congress shall make no law respecting an establishment of religion, or prohibiting the free exercise thereof." Through its free exercise clause, the First Amendment protects the individual's right to freedom of conscience and free expression of religious beliefs. Belief is not the same as action.

The government clearly has the ability to prevent certain actions that might endanger people. The Supreme Court ultimately decides how to interpret the meaning of the establishment clause but its decisions frequently leads to controversy. There have been instances when the courts have permitted a state to take custody of a sick minor if the parents, for religious reasons, refuse to have the child receive adequate medical attention that could save the child's life. After the child receives proper care, the court will then return the child to the parents. Some of the Supreme Court decisions dealt with financial aid to religious organizations, funding transportation for students attending religious schools, the funding of textbooks, and special education projects. In the United States there is no wall separating church and state. Contrary to popular belief, there is nothing in the Constitution that says anything about "a wall of separation." The fact of the matter is that although religion has always been an important part of American life, it has often caused controversy. Disputants frequently go to the Supreme Court to settle disputes about where to draw the line between church and state.

EXCLUSIONARY RULE

The exclusionary rule is a legal principle that prohibits law enforcement officials from introducing illegally obtained evidence in a trial. The rule is to protect a defendant's Constitutional rights. The rule has nothing to do with whether a defendant is guilty or not. The rule deals with how officials obtain evidence to help convict a defendant. Critics of the rule claim it permits those that might be guilty of a crime to go free because of a possible minor legal infraction. In the past, if a search warrant had an incorrect date, judges could throw out any evidence obtained because of that minor error. The Supreme Court introduced the "good faith" rule in 1984. It permits the introduction of evidence even if was obtained by an inadvertent error such as an incorrect date. The collection of evidence to use in a trial is a complicated matter. For example, if the police stop a car for a speeding violation can they then search the car for drugs. Car searches have caused the courts to hand down many rulings, some of which have been contradictory.

EXECUTIVE AGREEMENTS

The president has the authority to negotiate executive agreements with foreign governments. Unlike treaties, executive agreements do not require Senate ratification. These agreements ordinarily deal with routine issues but presidents can abuse this power. They may decide on an executive agreement if they believe the Senate might not support a treaty. Examples of major issues treated as executive agreements include the 1940 destroyer-base deal with Great Britain. Some members of the Senate believed the agreement violated America's neutrality during the early stages of WW II. They did not want the United States to become involved in the European war. Some critics think the two presidents, Roosevelt and Truman, should have submitted the 1945 Yalta and Potsdam agreements to the Senate for ratification. The presidents, to avoid controversy and possible rejection, decided to deal with them as executive agreements despite their enormous importance. When President Roosevelt returned from the Yalta conference, he kept parts of the Yalta agreement secret. President Nixon did not seek Senate ratification of the 1973 Vietnam peace treaty. Critics oppose treating important agreements as executive agreements rather than treaties. They insist the Senate should have the opportunity to evaluate agreements and then vote on ratification. The ratification process has several functions including the Senate's ability to check the power of the executive branch. Senate debates may help clarify issues as well as helping to legitimatize an agreement, if approved. When the president fails to submit important issues to the Senate in treaty form, the assumption is he may be trying to conceal something controversial.

EXECUTIVE OFFICE OF THE PRESIDENT (EOP)

The presidency is a complex institution composed of many parts. In 1939, President Roosevelt established the Executive Office of the President (EOP). It consists of more than a dozen agencies and more than two thousand employees. The EOP includes the Council of Economic Advisors, the Domestic Policy Council, the Office of Management and Budget, Office of the First Lady, and many others. The various units of the EOP help formulate and implement policies. Important policy makers make frequent appearances before congressional committees in the House and Senate. Congress conducts these hearings to enable it to evaluate policies. The hearings may also serve as a check on the executive branch. Members of Congress may ask policy makers to explain and justify policies. Only the top individuals with the most responsibility in the EOP have access to the president. The Executive Office and the White House Office are sometimes confused but the two are distinct.

EXECUTIVE ORDERS

An executive order is simply a command by the president ordering some agency to take certain actions often in relation to legislation. Executive orders have the full force of law. Some executive orders have been controversial because of the importance of the subject. President Roosevelt issued an executive order that resulted in the internment of more than 100,000 Japanese during World War II despite the fact there was no indication they threatened the country in any way. The internment occurred at a time when many Japanese-Americans were serving in the military to help defend the country. In 1948, President Truman used an executive order to end segregation in the military. One reason why he relied on his executive power was the ability of southern Senators to prevent the passage of legislation ending segregation in the armed forces.

EXECUTIVE PRIVILEGE

Executive privilege is the ability of the president to withhold information from Congress or the courts. Presidents invoke executive privilege to protect confidentiality. Advisors must be confident that when they advise the president on sensitive subjects, the advice is confidential. They want assurance that opponents will not force the president to reveal the content of confidential conversations. The advice may deal with someone's character defects or unethical or immoral behavior. The president may invoke executive privilege because of concerns about national security. President Nixon defined executive privilege more expansively than any of his predecessors. During the Watergate scandal, he wanted to withhold certain incriminating information from a congressional committee and the courts but the Supreme Court ruled against him. The information, when it became public, led to his resignation in 1974. The Constitution does not mention executive privilege but the precedent dates back to George Washington. Invoking executive privilege frequently leads to conflict with the Congress because information is a source of power. The right to invoke executive privilege is a part of the separation of powers between and among the three branches of government. The president may refuse to make information available to a court if it involves national security. The court must then decide if the refusal is legally justified. The president and Congress can usually reach some accommodation to resolve executive privilege issues. President Clinton invoked executive privilege fourteen times. President George

W. Bush invoked it six times. President Obama invoked executive privilege only once during his first term in office but it caused a major controversy. It occurred during his reelection campaign. The timing made it difficult to resolve the issue.

EX POST FACTO

Ex post facto laws are laws that retroactively make an act illegal that was legal when committed. The Constitution specifically prohibits ex post facto laws. The prohibition is in Article I, Section 9 of the Constitution.

FACEBOOK

Facebook is a social networking website that has become an important political tool. It is also an important fund raising vehicle that enables political candidates to raise money and connect with supporters from different parts of the country. Facebook enables presidential candidates to get messages out to their supporters quickly and easily and it is especially important for connecting with young voters. Facebook is one of the many new tools in the information revolution that politicians are eager to exploit.

FAITH-BASED INITIATIVES

President George W. Bush initiated faith-based programs to permit religious organizations to participate in government-backed programs supported with tax funds. Religious organizations that sponsor programs such as drug rehabilitation, family counseling, youth programs and others can seek government funding. Helping a drug addict deal with addiction does not necessarily rely on religious values but opponents claim that policies may in fact reflect religious values. They argue this violates the establishment clause of the First Amendment. Supporters claim their programs do not directly promote religious values. Faith-based organizations are not necessarily directly affiliated with a particular church but they may nevertheless infuse their policies with religious values. It is often difficult to differentiate the values of independent organizations and those of a particular church. After his election in 2008, President Obama supported some faith-based initiatives many Democrats opposed. He claimed his policies in support of faith-based initiatives did not contradict the idea of separation of church and state. He did not think the separation doctrine precluded cooperation between church and state. The American Civil Liberties Union disagreed. They thought policies carried out by church related organizations violated the First Amendment establishment clause.

FAST TRACK LEGISLATION

Fast track legislation is the willingness of Congress to accept or reject trade agreements negotiated by the executive branch without adding amendments. Congress can only approve or reject an agreement. Congress cannot amend fast track agreements. One reason for this process is to prevent states opposed to one or more provisions of a trade bill from trying to amend or kill the entire bill. Fast track legislation gives members of Congress some cover to protect them from angry constituents. Despite the cover, Congress is often reluctant to approve "fast track" legislation. Protecting constituents helps members of Congress win reelection. Some members wish to include in trade legislation provisions to help protect the environment or the right of workers to organize labor

unions. Members sometimes insert these provisions because they want to kill the legislation. Foreign governments do not want Congress telling them what they must do. It is a question of national sovereignty. Getting Congress to approve trade agreements is always difficult because such agreements are sometimes detrimental to some constituency although it may be beneficial to the country as a whole. Some members of Congress oppose fast track trade agreements because they do not like yielding their power in a way that benefits the executive branch. Congress first approved fast track in 1974. A president must seek congressional approval each time he wants trade legislation put on the fast track.

FEDERALISM

Before the adoption of the Constitution in 1789, each state in the confederation was sovereign. In 1781, the states completed ratification of the Articles of Confederation that recognized the sovereignty of each state. Sovereignty meant they controlled most of their own affairs without interference by the national government. Delegates at the Constitutional Convention decided to adopt a federal form of government. A good definition of federalism is the constitutional distribution of power between the national and state governments. It is also another aspect of checks and balances and separated powers. The definition of federalism is simple enough but the reality is much more complex. The national government exercises some powers, state governments exercise others, and both governments share some powers such as taxation. The national government exercises delegated powers. State governments exercise reserved powers. The national and state governments exercise shared or concurrent powers. The distribution of power within the federal system is dynamic and subject to change. In 1789, when the states approved the Constitution they possessed a great deal of power but this changed with the passing of time. The national government assumed more and more power vis-à-vis the states particularly after the Civil War. Some changes in the distribution of power are the result of developments since the adoption of the Constitution. There was little interstate commerce when delegates approved the Constitution but this changed as the economy grew and expanded and the means of transporting goods improved. Interstate commerce requires regulations for a variety of reasons including safety and health reasons. Although the power to regulate commerce takes up only one sentence in the Constitution, Congress and the courts can define commerce expansively to include "commercial activity." This definition enables the national government to regulate many things not usually associated with commerce including civil rights and criminal activities. Beginning in 1932, President Roosevelt's New Deal legislation further shifted the distribution of power in favor of the national government. Since 1936, many Supreme Court rulings have contributed to the increase of power at the national level. The globalization process is another factor that has enlarged the powers of the national government vis-à-vis the states. The federal system is complex because the flow of power between the national government and the states is multidirectional. Power flows in both directions concurrently but unevenly.

FEDERALISM: COOPERATIVE

Cooperative federalism is associated with the New Deal. After Roosevelt's election in 1932, he initiated a series of policies to promote cooperation between the national government and the states. Cooperative federalism became a substitute for dual federalism. The basic premise of cooperative federalism is shared responsibility but some critics claim the term is misleading because states and local units of government are the junior partners. The national government dominates the process. Congress decides on the programs and provides the financing but states are responsible for implementing the programs. Cooperative federalism is part of an ongoing problem of reconciling the distribution of powers between the national and state governments within the federal system.

FEDERALISM: DUAL

Dual federalism (also called layer cake federalism) deals with the distribution of power between the national and state governments. According to this theory, both the national and state governments are sovereign. Each has its own sphere of power protected by the Constitution. The national government is sovereign in some areas such as regulating interstate commerce but states have the power to regulate intrastate commerce. Until the Civil War, southern states supported dual federalism as a means to protect the system of slavery. Dual federalism helped shape the Supreme Court's 1857 Dred Scott decision. After the civil war, the Supreme Court continued to protect the power of states although it gradually accepted the growing role of the national government. The theory of dual federalism remained in force until the 1930s when President Roosevelt discarded the policy because the national government had to cope with the consequences of the 1929 economic crash. State governments did not have the resources to deal with all the problems stemming from the crash. The national government has one power states do not have, the power to print money. Disputants often call upon the Supreme Court to resolve conflicts between the states and the national government.

FEDERALISM: HORIZONAL

Horizontal federalism refers to the relationship states have with each other. It includes the Full Faith and Credit Clause of the Constitution, the Privileges and Immunities clause and the extradition clause. Interstate compacts such as the Delaware River Port Authority (Pennsylvania and New Jersey), Delaware River and Bay Authority (Delaware and New Jersey) and the Port Authority of New York and New Jersey are examples of horizontal federalism. Many states have cooperative relations with other states particularly neighboring states. There is often cooperation between agencies of two or more states to implement agreed upon programs. States often confront similar problems that can best be resolved by cooperation.

FEDERALISM: VERTICAL

Vertical federalism refers to the relationship between the national government and the states. Each level has its own distinct powers but some powers overlap. Vertical federalism refers to the obligations of both levels, national and state. The national government is obligated to protect the territorial integrity of the states. States are responsible for carrying out elections to determine who will serve in the Congress. The supremacy clause of the Constitution often favors the national government when it is involved in conflicts with the states. The Supreme Court must sometimes resolve conflicts between the two levels of government.

FEDERALIST PARTY

Federalist was the term that described individuals supporting the ratification of the Constitution. In 1789, the states successfully completed the ratification process. In 1792, those individuals adhering to federalist principles organized the Federalist Party. Alexander Hamilton played a major role in establishing the party. It supported a strong central government, sound fiscal policies, and better relations with Great Britain. The Federalist Party had the backing of plantation owners, wealthy merchants, and in general those in the upper economic class. Federalists supported a strong central government and sound financial policies including a national bank. Federalists included James Madison, John Jay, and others. George Washington supported Federalist programs but he was never a formal member of the party. He remained an independent. John Adams was the only Federalist elected president. The Federalists held together until about 1820 when the party dissolved for lack of support. The decline began with the election of Thomas Jefferson in 1800. He led the Democratic Republican Party that eventually became the Democratic Party. The Federalists supported the Alien and Sedition Acts that proved very unpopular with the voters and helped Thomas Jefferson win the 1800 presidential election. One of the major problems confronting the Federalists was the inability to attract voters other than those in the upper class. It never became a mass party. When the Federalist Party lost its support many members joined the Whig Party that eventually split over the slave issue. Many Whig Party supporters in the north then switched to the Republican Party.

FILIBUSTER

A filibuster is an attempt by a minority of members in the Senate to engage in prolonged debate to kill or significantly modify a bill they oppose. Supporters argue that majorities can be tyrannical or just simply wrong therefore the need for a right to filibuster. In the past, southern Senators often relied on the filibuster to prevent passage of civil rights legislation but Senators used the filibuster for other issues as well. The right to filibuster is part of the system of checks and balances. It is also a check on large majorities controlling the Senate although large majorities can come about only as a result of electoral outcomes. Supporters of the filibuster fear that political parties controlling a large majority could hastily pass legislation. In the past, some filibusters lasted for an extended period. To prolong debate, Senators would read food recipes into the record, recite Shakespeare, or read names from a telephone book. In 1957, a southern Senator, Strum Thurmond, spoke for a little more than twenty-four hours to kill a civil rights bill. When southerners lost their dominant role in the Senate, opponents instituted reforms to limit debate. The Senate can now end a filibuster by invoking cloture that requires a sixty-vote majority rather than the two-thirds vote needed in the past. Senators can no longer prolong debate by considering issues not relevant to the legislation. rather than the two-thirds vote needed in the past. Senators can no longer prolong debate by talking about issues not relevant to the legislation it is considering.

FISCAL POLICY

The government uses fiscal policies to help regulate the economy. Fiscal policy emphasizes tax and spending laws to help the economy expand or contract. During a downturn in the economy, government agencies put into place policies to encourage consumer spending. This usually involves more government spending to stimulate the economy. The government may also adopt tax policies to encourage consumer spending. These policies are associated with Keynesian economics that allegedly helped the country recover from the 1929 crash. The government would end the stimulative policies as the economy recovered. When the economy is expanding in a sustained way, the government should curb spending. Some economists dispute the effectiveness of fiscal policies to expand or contract the economy.

FOURTEENTH AMENDMENT

After the Civil War, Congress approved the 13th, 14th, and 15th amendments, the so-called Civil War amendments. The Fourteenth Amendment contains two important clauses, due process and equal protection. The Supreme Court has interpreted both clauses to broaden freedoms and to strike down laws and policies promoting or supporting discrimination. After 1936, the New Deal relied on the Fourteenth Amendment to bring about economic reforms the court had rejected in the past. The Supreme Court has interpreted the Fourteenth Amendment to bring about a fundamental redistribution power between the national and state governments in favor or the former. The court has also interpreted the Fourteenth Amendment to make most of the first ten amendments applicable to the states. The due process clause prohibits states from depriving people of life, liberty, or property unless they follow certain guidelines. The equal protection clause protects people against discriminatory policies. The Supreme Court relied on this clause to end the many forms of segregation put into place in the south after the civil war. The Court has also used the clause to prevent discriminatory treatment in areas other than segregation such as sex and age discrimination. Much of the 1954 ruling in Brown v. Board of Education relied on the equal protection clause of the Fourteenth Amendment. It declared unconstitutional policies based on the "separate but equal" doctrine. Southern states relied on this doctrine to enforce segregation laws. Over time, the Supreme Court incorporated many of the rights guaranteed in the Bill of Rights into the Fourteenth Amendment and then made these rights applicable to the states.

FREE EXERCISE CLAUSE

Among other things, the free exercise clause of the First Amendment deals with the issue of freedom of religion and its relationship to the Establishment Clause. The Supreme Court has ruled that governments cannot regulate religious beliefs but can regulate behavior. From the founding era of the United States until today, most Americans have agreed that individuals have the right to freely express their religious beliefs. During the colonial period, many people came to America because of the promise of religious freedom. The issue of church-state relations has always been contentious sometimes requiring the intervention of the Supreme Court to resolve differences. Supreme Court decisions may however generate additional controversies.

FULL FAITH AND CREDIT

The full faith and credit clause of the Constitution is located in Article IV, sec. 1. It requires states to respect the legal judgments of other states. When an individual commits a crime in one state and flees to another, that state is obligated to return the criminal to the state where the crime was committed. The full faith and credit clause pertains to things such as contracts "public acts, records, and judicial proceedings." The full faith and credit clause is an essential aspect of the American federalism but some aspects of the clause remain controversial. For example, some states refuse to recognize same sex marriages performed in other states. In the past, northern states would sometimes refuse to extradite a black person accused of a crime in a southern state. This might occur if the state believed that he or she would not receive a fair trial because of racial practices in the south. Disputes of this kind were not unusual but became much less important as a result of civil rights reforms of the 1960s.

GERRYMANDER

Gerrymandering is the process whereby the majority party in a state legislature creates electoral districts that helps assure the party of electoral advantages. Safe districts enable the majority party to save resources for use in more competitive districts. Electoral districts may vary in size and shape. A gerrymandered district reduces political party competition and denies voters a genuine choice of

FOURTEENTH AMENDMENT

After the Civil War, Congress approved the 13th, 14th, and 15th amendments, the so-called Civil War amendments. The Fourteenth Amendment contains two important clauses, due process and equal protection. The Supreme Court has interpreted both clauses to broaden freedoms and to strike down laws and policies promoting or supporting discrimination. After 1936, the New Deal relied on the Fourteenth Amendment to bring about economic reforms the court had rejected in the past. The Supreme Court has interpreted the Fourteenth Amendment to bring about a fundamental redistribution power between the national and state governments in favor or the former. The court has also interpreted the Fourteenth Amendment to make most of the first ten amendments applicable to the states. The due process clause prohibits states from depriving people of life, liberty, or property unless they follow certain guidelines. The equal protection clause protects people against discriminatory policies. The Supreme Court relied on this clause to end the many forms of segregation put into place in the south after the civil war. The Court has also used the clause to prevent discriminatory treatment in areas other than segregation such as sex and age discrimination. Much of the 1954 ruling in Brown v. Board of Education relied on the equal protection clause of the Fourteenth Amendment. It declared unconstitutional policies based on the "separate but equal" doctrine. Southern states relied on this doctrine to enforce segregation laws. Over time, the Supreme Court incorporated many of the rights guaranteed in the Bill of Rights into the Fourteenth Amendment and then made these rights applicable to the states.

GERRYMANDERING

Gerrymandering is the process whereby the majority party in a state legislature creates electoral districts that helps assure the party of electoral advantages. Safe districts enable the majority party to save resources for use in more competitive districts. Electoral districts may vary in size and shape. A gerrymandered district reduces political party competition and denies voters a genuine choice of party candidates. Correcting gerrymandered districts is difficult because the ruling party in a state legislature has the votes to create districts that favor the party. Minority or opposition parties often seek remedy in the court system. Some policy makers believe that Gerrymandered districts contribute to the gridlock in Washington. These districts often result in political polarization because they often disadvantage moderates in both parties. In 1812, Governor Elbridge Gerry signed a law that redrew electoral districts to favor his party, hence the term "gerrymander."

GLASS CEILING

Glass ceiling is a term that describes a process whereby an individual cannot make advancements such as promotion at work because of prejudice. The lack of advancement is because of invisible barriers rather than rules or regulations. The term applies to politics as well as business. Women and minorities are usually the victims of glass ceiling policies. Many of the invisible barriers are disappearing although not as quickly as some would like. In 2007, the House of Representatives elected Nancy Pelosi Speaker of the House, the first women to hold that position. Several states now have female governors. A number of women have run for the presidency but none have been successful nor have any been on the ticket of one of the major parties. In 1984, Walter Mondale persuaded the Democratic Party to nominate Geraldine Ferraro to run on the ticket as his vice president. They lost in forty nine of fifty states. Problems associated with the glass ceiling can be difficult to deal with because discrimination is often embedded in tradition.

GRANDFATHER CLAUSE

The grandfather clause was a device southern states employed after the Civil War to prevent blacks from voting. You were eligible to vote only if your grandfather had been eligible to vote. Blacks usually had no grandfathers eligible to vote because they were either slaves or not eligible to vote for other reasons. Some states used the grandfather clause to permit whites the right to vote even if they could not meet other voting qualifications such as property taxes or literacy tests. The grandfather clause was only one of several devices southerners developed to prevent blacks from voting. Other methods included things such as poll taxes and literacy tests. The 1964 Voting Rights Act abolished most of these devices and as a result, many blacks were eligible to vote. The number of blacks elected to political offices in the south substantially increased after 1964.

GREAT SOCIETY

The Great Society refers to the policies proposed by President Lyndon Johnson to extend and add to the programs associated with the New Deal. Some Great Society programs included Head Start, Medicare and the 1964 Civil Rights Act. Critics of the Great Society disliked the huge growth in government bureaucracies to deal with the many programs President Johnson supported. The Great Society programs combined with the Vietnam War created a huge budget deficit. The entitlement programs became more expensive as more people became eligible for their benefits. President Johnson failed to pay sufficient attention to the costs of the programs he neither supported nor was he concerned about budgetary deficits. Although he was eligible to do so, President Johnson decided not to seek reelection in 1968. His approval rating when he retired was just below 50%. His unpopularity was largely the result of the Vietnam War.

GRIDLOCK

Gridlock in Washington occurs when the executive and legislative branches of government cannot agree on programs and policies. This usually occurs when different political parties control the two branches of government. Gridlock may occur at different levels and within levels of government. Gridlock may characterize relations between the House and Senate, between committees in either house, or between Congress and the president. Gridlock between the parties may occur if the moderate faction in each party is weak. When this occurs, the right wing of the Republican Party and the left wing of the Democratic Party are usually the dominant factions. Some policy makers believe that term limits would help cure the problem of extreme partisanship but others disagree. Term limits might generate a different set of problems. Some critics believe that presidential leadership is the necessary antidote to gridlock. President Kennedy had difficulty getting Congress to approve many of his legislative proposals that became law after his assassination. President Johnson was able to do what President Kennedy could not.

GROUP OF TWENTY: G-20

The Group of Twenty consists of finance ministers and central bank governors from twenty of the most important nations dealing with economic issues. These are nations that have a significant impact on global economic trends. The Group of Twenty replaced the Group of Eight. The change from one group to another was in part a response to growing globalization trends with more countries having an impact on economic and financial conditions throughout the world. The leaders meet twice a year but consultations between and among the ministers take place on a regular basis. Members realize their economic policies may have a global as well as a national impact therefore the need for greater cooperation. The main concern of the G-20 is to put into place policies that contribute to sustained economic growth globally.

HARD MONEY/SOFT MONEY

Two components of campaign funding are hard money and soft money. Policy makers define hard money as money spent by supporters to help elect a particular candidate. Federal campaign finance laws regulate the amount of money contributed to elect an individual. Soft money may be contributed to a political party or an organization for any of numerous purposes such as helping to register voters, getting out the vote on election day, or to support or oppose a particular issue. The government does not regulate soft money. Differentiating between hard and soft money can be difficult. Soft money may be spent to help get out the vote of a particular set of voters who are likely to vote for a particular candidate. Groups generally have a specific targeted audience for registering voters or getting out the vote. Regulating campaign finances is difficult because lawyers are generally able to find loopholes in the regulations. Efforts to better control campaign spending is always difficult. Electoral campaigns at all levels of government have become increasingly expensive.

HOUSE OF REPRESENTATIVES: SPEAKER

The Speaker of the House leads the majority party in the House of Representatives. The power of the Speaker depends on several things including what political party controls the White House, the size of the majority in the House, relations with the president, and the Speaker's leadership skills. The political culture of the House also helps determine the power and influence of the Speaker. He must be deferential to the needs of party members but he must also impose some discipline on members to ensure a successful legislative record. The House elects the Speaker every two years. He or she influences the legislative calendar to reflect the priorities of his political party. The Speaker is often the president's main opponent if they are not in the same party. In addition to all his other functions, he must also represent the legislative district that elects him to Congress.

IDENTITY POLITICS

Identity politics refers to policies that affect a particular group based on things such as sex, religion, or race. Affirmative action policies are an example of identity politics. The government may confer some advantages on minorities to compensate for past discriminatory policies. Critics of identity politics fear that policies that seek to favor one group over another leads to political fragmentation and divisiveness. Identity politics is sometimes associated with political correctness and multiculturalism. If you say that someone in the Mafia is Italian, the politically correct guardians expect you to immediately add that not all Italians are members of the Mafia. It is not clear why anyone would make that assumption.

IDEOLOGY

Ideology is basically a set of ideas based on values. Ideology may help individuals evaluate history, may suggest a program for the future, or may win a political candidate popular support. An ideology provides individuals with a compass for judging and advocating policies. Fascism was a popular ideology in the 1930s and helped bring about World War II. After the war, communism was popular in some parts of the world and became a major cause of international conflict. Leaders in democratic political systems interpret ideological beliefs in a moderate fashion designed to win the support of a majority of voters. There is often a huge difference between the ideas contained in an ideology and their implementation. Leaders often fail to translate ideals that sound good in the abstract into practical policy. Human nature has a way of intervening. Although the Republican and Democratic parties support policies based on their ideologies both are also pragmatic. Pragmatism usually requires a degree of moderation that encourages the two parties to cooperate with each other. Pragmatism and ideology may conflict with each other.

IMPEACHMENT

The delegates at the Constitutional Convention decided Congress could impeach the president and other federal officials if there was good reason for doing so. The Constitution does not define the meaning of an impeachable offense but it does intentionally make the process difficult. Delegates at the convention wanted to make certain that efforts to remove officials, including the president, were not the result of policy disagreements or conflicting political views. The impeachment process has two stages. Impeachment is technically a list of charges made by the Judiciary Committee in the House of Representatives. This is similar to an indictment in a criminal case. If the Judiciary Committee approves the charges, it submits them to the House for a vote. A majority of the House must approve each charge. After approving the charges, the House then sends them to the Senate. It then conducts a trial to determine if the individual is guilty or innocent. A two-thirds vote is required for removing an individual from office. If the House impeaches the president and the Senate finds him guilty, he is removed from office and may subsequently be prosecuted if crimes have been committed. The House of Representatives impeached two presidents, Andrew Johnson in 1868 and Bill Clinton in 1998 but the Senate did not vote for expulsion. The House of Representatives drew up a list of impeachment charges against President Nixon in 1974 but he resigned before the impeachment vote. Although congressional leaders try to make the impeachment process as objective as possible, some members are motivated by political factors. Republicans controlled the House of Representatives when it voted to impeach President Clinton in 1998. The House of Representatives voted to impeach President Johnson because they disapproved of the post-civil war policies he supported. When Congress impeaches a president or other officials and removes them from office, there is no right of appeal. The Justice Department may indict officials even if no impeachment occurs.

IMPLIED POWERS

The implied powers are those powers related to the expressed powers in Article I, Section 8 of the Constitution. Powers not specifically listed in the Constitution may be justified by the necessary and proper clause or a number of other clauses. The national income tax and military drafts are examples of policies approved by the government based on implied powers. These powers are frequently controversial because of the difficulty of determining the justification for a particular policy. Conservatives and liberals often disagree on what constitutes an implied power. Determining what the Constitution implies is often a prudential judgment that may have to be resolved by the courts.

IMPRESSMENT

One of the causes for the War of 1812 was the British policy of impressment. British warships would cause American ships to halt at sea. The British would then board the ship and "capture" any sailors that could not prove they were American citizens. This policy of impressment angered the American people and helped bring about the War of 1812.

INCORPORATION DOCTRINE

When the states ratified the Bill of Rights, they were applicable to the national government but not to the states. Delegates to the Constitutional Convention assumed the national government was more likely to abuse the rights of people than state governments. The Civil War brought about a redistribution of power between the two levels of government. Some officials thought it was time to make the Bill of Rights applicable to the states. The Supreme Court brought about the changes by relying upon various parts of the Fourteenth Amendment ratified after the Civil War. Over a period of time most but not all of the first ten amendments were selectively incorporated into the Fourteenth Amendment and made applicable to the states. The result was a significant redistribution of power that favored the national government at the expense of the states. This process continued after Roosevelt's election in 1932 because many Americans believed only the national government had adequate resources to deal with the economic problems confronting the country. Financially, the states were unable to cope with the consequences of the 1929 economic crash. Under Roosevelt, the national government began to do many things that would have been unconstitutional in the past. After 1936, the Supreme Court interpreted the Constitution in a way that permitted the expansion of government power at the national level. Critics of the incorporation doctrine believe it compromised the intention of the founding fathers. They deliberately created a political system to limit the power of the national government.

INCUMBENT

An incumbent is an individual who occupies a political office. Incumbents often win reelection because they have name recognition and access to more resources, including funding. The reelection rate for incumbents in the House and Senate is approximately 90%. The high reelection rate contributes to the growing partisanship in Congress. Every ten years state legislatures create safe seats for their political party. This further reduces competition between the parties but may increase competition within the party. If a Democrat is challenged in the primaries, the challenge will usually come from the left wing of the party. Challenges to Republican incumbents usually come from the right. This results in growing polarization between the two parties thus making it more difficult to reach compromise decisions.

INTEREST GROUPS

Interest groups and political parties both attempt to influence government policies. The difference between the two is that political parties, through the electoral system, try to organize the government. Interest groups do not. Interest group activity is a form of representation that serves as a link between people or certain groups of people and the government. The First Amendment that protects speech and the right to petition the government protects their activities. Many interest groups operate at all levels of decision-making, executive, legislative, and judicial. They may also operate at the national, state, and local levels of government. There are many types of interest groups representing varied interests and they often play an essential role in the government's decision-making process. Interest groups are involved in many political and government functions. Among other things, they play an educational role in promoting or opposing legislation. They help inform legislators and the public about a particular issue although they do it in a way that best protects the interest of the group. Interest groups may also attempt to influence foreign policy making. Foreign governments may create interest groups to promote their policy preferences. There is no dispute that interest groups wield an enormous influence on government decisions. Critics charge they wield too much influence but interest groups are only as powerful as Congress allows them to be. Members do not have to vote the way lobbyists want them to but interest groups have an array of instruments to influence congressional voting including huge sums of money. Some interest groups operate primarily within one or the other political party. Labor unions, for example, are generally identified with the Democratic Party and the election of Democrats. Corporations frequently identify with the Republican Party. Interest groups may buy television ads, help get out the vote, or help fund political campaigns. There are thousands of interest groups dealing with many topics. They represent various interests including professional organizations, trade groups, social issues, charitable organizations, labor unions, churches, sports, and many others. Some groups organize around a specific issue but others have multiple interests. Some groups seek to influence a particular branch of government such as the legislature or the courts but many operate at several government levels. Lobbyist is the term for individuals representing the interest groups. Foreign governments hire lobbyists to protect their interests because America's policies may affect their wellbeing in vital ways. States, cities, and local governments also hire lobbyists to influence the national government particularly when it comes to the distribution of funds. Interest groups not only attempt to influence policymakers, they also try to influence public opinion by advertising on television and other media. They frequently have a speaker's bureau and use their personnel to address audiences often without charge. Some interest groups contribute money to both political parties to enable them to access policymakers regardless of which party wins the election. If a member of Congress is defeated or decides to retire, he or she may then go to work for an interest group. These groups are usually eager to hire former members of Congress because they know how Congress works, are familiar with the sources of power in relation to a particular issue, and have access to former colleagues. Access is a source of power.

IRON TRIANGLE

In politics, the three parts of the iron triangle are congressional committees, government agencies (bureaucracy), and interest groups. Critics allege the three groups that make up the triangle exercise a disproportionate amount of power over congressional legislation and government regulations. Bureaucrats and members of Congress that leave the government frequently find employment with interest groups. These individuals generally have easy access to their former colleagues. Access is an important aspect of power. Members of a congressional committee, including staff, may plan eventually to work for a corporation or an interest group doing business with the committee. There are government regulations attempting to deal with this situation but individuals often circumvent the rules. When members of Congress approve legislation desired by an interest group, it will usually repay the member by contributing to his reelection campaign. The aid may come in many forms. The interaction of the three parts of the triangle occurs at many levels of the decision making process. The term "iron triangle" suggests that the connection of the three parts is too strong to be broken.

JAY TREATY

The United States Senate ratified the Jay Treaty in 1794. The primary purpose of the treaty was to resolve difference between the United States and Great Britain, some of which dated back to the Revolutionary War. By the terms of the Jay Treaty, Great Britain agreed to withdraw its forces from some lands it occupied since before the Revolutionary War. The two sides agreed to submit to arbitration disputes over the wartime debts and the territorial boundary with Canada. The treaty generated a great deal of debate between those supporting the treaty, the Federalists, and those opposing it, the Anti-Federalists. President Washington led the fight for ratification; Thomas Jefferson led the opposition. The ratification dispute did much to establish the two major political parties at the time, the Federalists and the Democratic Republicans. The Federalists supported the treaty because they wanted to resolve differences with Great Britain and reduce the possibility of another war. Great Britain was eager to resolve differences with the United States to discourage it from going to war on the side of the French. Thomas Jefferson and the Anti-Federalists supported France and wanted to do all they could to aid the French cause. The Jay Treaty gave the United States an opportunity to develop its resources and power in preparation for future crisis. President Washington supported the treaty because one of his primary foreign policy goals was to keep the United States out of European wars and the concentrate on the development and growth of the American economy.

JOINT CONGRESSIONAL COMMITTEE

Joint committees are composed of members of the House and Senate. There are four permanent joint committees: Joint Committee on Printing, Joint Committee on Taxation, Joint Committee on the Library, and the Joint Economic Committee that deals with important economic issues. The other joint committees deal with housekeeping measures such as management and budget questions. From time to time, Congress will create temporary joint committees such as the Joint Committee on the Organization of Congress. When these committees complete their tasks they are disbanded.

JUDICIARY ACT 1789

In 1789, Congress approved the Judiciary Act establishing the American federal court system composed of three tiers, the Supreme Court, Appellate Courts, and district courts. Each of the three has its own jurisdiction. Delegates at the 1787 Constitutional Convention did not devote much attention to the judicial system. They thought it would be the least important of the three branches of government. Article III established the Supreme Court but delegates said little about its composition, membership, or jurisdiction. This duty fell to the first Congress that met in 1789. Congress determines the number of courts, both trial and appellate, and determines the number of Supreme Court judges. Initially the Supreme Court had six judges but since 1869, there have been nine judges. George Washington appointed John Jay the first Chief Justice. The 1789 Judiciary Act also created the office of Attorney General. The Anti-Federalists wanted to limit the number of courts and their jurisdiction. They wanted the court system to be primarily under the control of the states, not the national government. They disliked the idea of appointing judges rather than have them elected and they opposed life tenure. They feared a strong judicial system would endanger individual rights because judges would be appointed, not elected. Anti-Federalists preferred a weak federal judicial system but they lost the battle. The Judiciary Act did not give the Supreme Court the power judicial review. The Court assumed that power in Marbury v. Madison 1803.

JUDICIAL ACTIVISM

Judicial activism generally supports the idea that political opinions and values are part of the law that judges should not ignore. Judicial activism is the practice of issuing broad decisions influenced by factors other than relevant legal doctrines. Critics accuse judicial activists of deciding on an opinion and then finding a justification to support it. Liberals and conservatives accuse each other of judicial activism when they disagree with a particular court ruling, especially the Supreme Court. Activists respond by pointing out that conditions change with the passing of time and judges must sometimes reinterpret parts of the Constitution. This is in keeping with the idea of a "living Constitution." Critics generally cite the 1973 Roe v. Wade decision as an example of judicial activism because the Constitution says nothing about the right of abortion. The majority relied on the protection of privacy to justify their decision. The right to privacy is sufficiently broad to justify a great many things.

JUDICIAL RESTRAINT

Judicial restraint is the opposite of judicial activism. Advocates of judicial restraint believe the Supreme Court should not declare a legislative act unconstitutional unless there is overwhelming evidence to do so. Judicial restraint relies on precedents to guide the **decision-making process. Judges supporting judicial restraint** oppose rulings such as Roe v. Wade that legalized the right to abortion. They also oppose that part of the ruling dividing pregnancy into three cycles to determine when an abortion could take place. Critics claim this was an example of making rather than interpreting the law.

KENNEDY ASSASSINATION

On November 22, 1963, Lee Harvey Oswald assassinated President John F. Kennedy in Dallas, Texas. Lyndon Johnson then became president. He completed Kennedy's term and then defeated Barry Goldwater in the 1964 presidential race. Texas Governor Connally was in the car with President Kennedy and was seriously wounded in the attack but survived. There have been numerous attempts to kill presidents or those elected but not yet inaugurated. In 1981, an assassin seriously injured President Reagan. A great many people are involved in trying to protect the president but his many public appearances make him vulnerable.

KENNEDY-NIXON DEBATES

In the 1960 presidential campaign, John F. Kennedy and Richard Nixon participated in four televised debates. This was not the first time presidential candidates debated but the first time they debated on television. The debates played an important role in the election outcome. Experts agree they helped John F. Kennedy in part because he was more telegenic than Nixon. The debates also enabled Kennedy to effectively deal with the issue of his youth. Nixon charged that Kennedy was too young and politically inexperienced to effectively lead the country. In the debates, Kennedy conveyed the impression he was knowledgeable about the important issues despite his relative lack of experience. There were no other presidential debates until Carter-Ford debates in 1976. Since then debates have taken place every four years. Critics disagree on the impact debates have on voting behavior. They generally agree the debates give voters an opportunity to judge the television personality of the candidates but they are less useful on policy issues because candidates are sometimes vague about their policy preferences. Useful or not, candidates must enter the debates to have a chance of winning the nomination or the election. Presidential debates may have one of two outcomes. One candidate is outstanding and this contributes to victory. The other outcome is that a candidate does so badly that his opponent wins the election by default. During the debates, candidates must be careful about what they say because critics can make a minor error seem significant. Debates have become increasingly important in the nomination process but they often take on the characteristics of a comedy show. It is difficult to have a serious debate when there are six or more participants.

KNOW NOTHING PARTY

The Know Nothing Party, organized in 1849, changed its name in 1854 to the American Party. It built its reputation on things it disliked rather than things it favored. It opposed immigration and was particularly antagonistic towards Catholics. Among other things, it wanted to prevent Catholics from teaching in public schools. Many members of the party believed that Catholics wanted the Pope to govern America but they were not clear how he was to accomplish this.

In response to questions about their party beliefs, followers responded by saying "I don't know." The party had some electoral success but failed to win approval for legislation that implemented their ideas and beliefs. By the 1850s, immigration was less significant than the slavery issue. By the time of the Civil War, the American Party ceased being a significant political force in American politics.

LAME DUCK

Lame duck refers to an officeholder who is defeated in an election but remains in office until his or her successor is installed. The term also applies to a two-term president after the election of his successor. The election takes place in November but the president remains in office until January. The term has no precise meaning. Some observers think a president becomes a lame duck at the beginning of his second term because he cannot run for a third term. The term implies a loss of power and influence.

LAYERCAKE FEDERALISM

See FEDERALISM: DUAL

LEGITIMACY

Legitimacy is an important concept in political science but it does not have a specific definition. An individual's values usually help determine whether a policy is legitimate or not. A politician would be in trouble if most people believe that something he or she has done is illegitimate. Some Senate Republicans decided to vote to impeach President Nixon because he told them lies. A president lying to members of Congress, particularly those that are in his political party, is illegitimate even if it is not illegal. What is or is not legitimate is subject to change. At one time, a divorced individual could not be a serious presidential candidate because many people considered divorce to be illegitimate.

LIBERALISM

Liberalism has a different meaning now than in the past. Until the inauguration of the New Deal in 1932, liberals believed that limited government was the best way to protect individual freedoms. Since 1932, liberals have supported intrusive government programs and government regulations they believed would improve the quality of life. The New Deal ushered in the era of the welfare state and more intrusive government policies. The government would provide safety nets to help protect people's basic needs. Safety net programs include such things as social security, worker's compensation, and a minimum wage. Liberals usually support programs designed to promote equality of results. Affirmative action programs allegedly help achieve this objective. Liberals believe that social and economic problems often require government assistance to help solve these problems. Although there is not always a clear demarcation line, liberals and conservatives are usually on opposite sides when dealing with issue such abortion, the role of religion in American life, welfare policies, and foreign policies. Liberals, much more than conservatives, are likely to support international organizations such as the United Nations. In presidential elections, the Republican and the Democratic parties need to appeal to Middle America and therefore tend not to emphasize ideology other than in a general way.

LIBERTARIANISM

Libertarianism is an ideology that emphasizes individual freedoms and democratic government with limited powers. They believe in maximum freedom and minimum government. Libertarianism overlaps with conservatism although the two are sometimes at odds. Conservatives frequently support regulation of behavior based on moral values but libertarians do not. They oppose legislating morality and this puts them at odds with conservatives. Libertarians support a foreign policy of non-intervention and reduced military budgets. They also support the legalization of many drugs and gay marriage. As individuals, libertarians may oppose things such as gay marriage but they oppose government's effort to regulate such institutions. There is a Libertarian Party but it has never been a major influence in shaping legislation or determining electoral outcomes. In presidential elections, libertarian candidates are insignificant actors that generally receive less than one percent of the popular vote. The party does function in all fifty states.

LINE ITEM VETO

A line item veto gives an executive the power not to implement portions of a legislative act without rejecting the entire act. Some governors have this power but the president does not. In 1996, Congress passed a bill giving the president the power to veto particular parts of a bill but two years later the Supreme Court declared the law unconstitutional.

LOBBYISTS

Lobbyists represent interest groups. The primary function of a lobbyist is to try and win congressional or government support for whatever programs his group is advocating. They also lobby bureaucrats to influence their rule making and implementation functions. Lobbyists are familiar with the way government and its many institutions work. They are experts in their field and knowledgeable about exploiting the levers of power in Washington. Some members of Congress, when they retire or are defeated, become lobbyists. Organizations are eager to hire former members of the legislative branch because they often have easy access to individuals they worked with while in Congress.

LOG CABIN REPUBLICANS

Log Cabin Republicans are a group of gay and lesbian Republicans that support the basic principles of the Republican Party but seek to promote the rights of homosexuals. Log Cabin Republicans are often at odds with the national leadership of the party because of its support for policies gays and lesbians consider unfair or unjust. The name, Log Cabin Republicans, was intended to identify the group with the ideals associated with President Lincoln but this has not worked as well as they hoped. Some Republicans have tried to disassociate themselves from the group. In 1995, Bob Dole, the Republican nominee for president, returned a one thousand dollar check the Log Cabin Republicans had contributed to his presidential campaign. Dole feared that identification with the Log Cabin Republicans would harm his electoral chances. Since 1995, gays and lesbians have become much more active politically although it is difficult to measure their influence. The homosexual vote generally supports the Democratic Party rather than Republicans. Homosexuals also contribute much more money to the Democratic Party. In 2010, in response to demands of gay and lesbian groups, President Obama abolished the Don't Ask Don't Tell policy. He wanted to eliminate any restrictions on gays serving in the military. There are Log Cabin Republican offices in all fifty states and Washington D.C.

LOUISIANA PURCHASE 1803

In 1803, President Jefferson's decision to purchase Louisiana from France was one of the great events in American history. The original plan was to offer France $10 million for New Orleans. France offered to sell the entire region for $15 million, a decision that shocked the Americans because it was so advantageous to the United States. President Jefferson, a strict constructionist, digressed from his own principles and greatly expanded the powers of the presidency by making the purchase. Nothing in the Constitution specifically authorized such power. The purchase was important because it reduced the possibility of war between France and the United States. At the time, the United States was militarily weak and had difficult relations with Great Britain, Spain, Canada, and various Indian tribes. The purchase was also important because it doubled the territorial size of the country. The Louisiana Purchase included parts or all of fourteen states. The territory included in the purchase makes up almost a quarter of the country today. The cost was about four cents an acre. The Louisiana Purchase was a major historical event that enabled the United States to become a world power. The purchase exacerbated the slave problem and complicated relations with the Indian tribes. In some ways, the purchase made the Civil War inevitable and doomed the Indian tribes to American domination.

MEANS TEST

A means test is the requirement that individuals seeking government aid must meet certain standards to determine eligibility. Some government programs require a means test including those dealing with various forms of welfare, medical care, education benefits, food stamps, and many others. Government programs such as Social Security are not means based. Individuals are automatically entitled to receive benefits once they reach a certain age regardless of their wealth. Support for means testing has become more acceptable as a result of government financial difficulties. Proponents of means testing would like to see it applied to more government policies as a way of saving money.

MEDIA: ROLE OF

The media has multiple roles in a democratic political system. Media outlets influence a nation's political culture, help shape public opinion about policy issues, and may act as a check on the abuse of governmental power. Measuring the influence of the media is difficult because there are now many media outlets. The print media is no longer as significant as it once was. Cable television has diminished the role of the three major networks, NBC, CBS, and ABC. People now get much of their information from outlets such as Facebook, Tweeter, and the internet in general. Major newspapers such as The New York Times and the Wall Street Journal have lost some of their influence and are no longer as economically profitable as they once were. TV personalities such as Jon Stewart and Stephen Colbert provide their opinions about political issues and candidates seeking office but they do so in a humorous context. Their primary function is entertaining audiences and maintaining their ratings but they do shape public opinion.

MISSOURI COMPROMISE 1820

The 1820 Missouri Compromise made evident the contentiousness of the slavery issue. The territory acquired as a result of the Louisiana Purchase compelled the Congress to deal with issues that would influence the future of slavery in America. By the terms of the 1820 compromise, Congress admitted Maine as a free state and Missouri as a slave state. The debate generated by the compromise made it clear that the contentious issue of slavery would continue as more territories became eligible for statehood. The strong feelings of those opposing or approving slavery indicated that the issue would continue to be divisive. The idea that slavery could cause a civil war was not new. As far back as the Constitutional Convention, it was evident that the slavery issue could lead to violence.

MODERN PRESIDENCY

The modern presidency dates from Franklin Roosevelt although some historians, for good reason, believe Theodore Roosevelt is a better choice. Since the 1929 economic recession and the emergence of the United States as the dominant world power after 1945, most Americans look to the president for leadership and guidance. The Congress cannot exercise leadership because of its size, structure, divisions, and procedures. The information revolution, including television and the electronic media, enables the president to communicate directly with the American people as often as he wishes. The president has many roles. He is the party leader, helps determine legislative priorities, and is the head of state as well as the political leader of the country. Even when he is not directly communicating with the people, the media covers his every activity. He is also in communication with leaders around the world. The modern president is, whether he welcomes the role or not, a world leader because many of his policies affect other nations in either a positive or negative way. In 1963, the United States and the Soviet Union agreed to establish a "hot line" to enable the leaders of both countries to communicate with each other in case of an emergency. The superpowers accepted the "hot line" because they knew that if they went to war it would be difficult to limit the fighting thus increasing the possibility of a nuclear exchange that could involve other nations. Modern means of transportation enables the president to meet with leaders anywhere in the world, on short notice. There are also regularly scheduled summit meetings of world leaders dealing with a variety of topics. For example, the leaders of the G-20 nations meet regularly to discuss common economic problems and propose solutions. Critics of presidential power believe the office has become too powerful. One obvious example of the growth of presidential power is the ability to dispatch troops abroad without first getting congressional approval. In confronting a crisis, Congress will sometimes pass a resolution couched in general terms that the president will use as justification for sending troops into combat. Some members of Congress may then complain they did not authorize dispatching troops to fight a war but such complaints do little good.

NATIONAL SECURITY COUNCIL

In 1947, Congress established the National Security Council to organize and formulate America's response to national security problems. At that time, the cold war was emerging as a major problem for American foreign policy makers. President Truman wanted the best advice to deal with cold war issues. Many agencies in Washington contribute to the foreign policy process including the State Department, the Central Intelligence Agency, Congress, the Department of Defense and many others. The national government needed an agency to give foreign policy some coherence. The president appoints the National Security Director who must then win Senate confirmation. The National Security Council grew in importance during the cold war because of the fact that there are always foreign policy conflicts the president must cope with. The president relies on the National Security Council to do things the State Department cannot do. The council can do things quickly and with much less publicity than the State Department but the president must now cope with the problem of controlling a huge national security bureaucracy. In addition to the National Security Council, many other agencies in Washington deal with national security issues either directly or indirectly. Conflicts between the National Security Council and other agencies dealing with foreign policy is not unusual. These conflicts often require the president's intervention.

NATURAL LAW

Natural law is allegedly valid everywhere because it is not man-made such as positive law. Natural law influenced many of Thomas Jefferson's ideas that he included in the Declaration of Independence. Many of the rights contained in the Declaration are God given rights that governments did not confer and therefore cannot take away. Critics sometimes rely on natural law to evaluate positive law, also called man made laws.

NECESSARY AND PROPER CLAUSE

SEE ELEASTIC CLAUSE

NEW DEAL

Franklin Roosevelt won the 1932 presidential election. His victory ushered in the era of the New Deal. Historians use the term to describe the set of policies Roosevelt put into place to cope with the consequences of the 1929 economic crash. After his election in 1932, he was immediately confronted with a host of complicated problems that seemed to defy solution. The country desperately needed leadership and the right mix of policies to begin an economic recovery. In his acceptance speech at the 1932 Democratic National Convention Roosevelt pledged to initiate a "new deal" for the American people. The expression has no exact meaning but is a symbol for the many economic and social reform programs associated with his presidency. He wanted to identify the Democratic Party with the "common man." He did this by proposing many reforms carried out by government agencies and he also initiated a number of entitlement programs to help people deal with their problems. He relied on deficit spending to help cope with the consequences of the 1929 crash. Ever since the New Deal, the American government has had much more control over the economy than in the past. New Deal policies greatly expanded the powers of the national government and those of the president. People now look to the government and to the president to help cope with problems confronting the nation. That is one of the many legacies of the New Deal. Another legacy is deficit spending that has become a major problem in part because the president and Congress failed to adequately fund programs they put into place. That situation can go on only for so long. Eventually, someone must pay the bills.

NEW DEAL ELECTORAL COALITION

The New Deal coalition refers to the voting groups the Democrats put together to win the 1932 presidential election. Before the election, the country was overwhelmingly Republican. The New Deal coalition consisted of labor unions, ethnic and racial minorities, southern whites, African Americans, liberals, farmers, intellectuals, and big city political machines. The coalition remained intact until the 1960s although Republicans did elect the president in 1952 and 1956. Some of President Johnson's policies contributed to the fracturing of the New Deal coalition. In the 1964 presidential election, Barry Goldwater, the Republican Party nominee, lost badly but did well in the southern states that previously were solidly Democratic. Another element that contributed to the end of the New Deal coalition was the fact that the big city political machines lost their luster and their ability to deliver the vote. Today, coalitions tend to be temporary. Voting blocs may change from one election to the next. One reason for this is that more voters now identify themselves as independent. They are no longer loyal to one political party.

NEW JERSEY PLAN

Delegates at the Constitutional Convention had to deal with the contentious issue of representation. They had strong opinions about the issue because it would help determine the ability of states to influence legislation. The New Jersey Plan was one of several plans put forth at the Constitutional Convention to deal with the representation issue. Proponents of this plan wanted to protect the power and influence of small states. They supported retaining the one house legislature but with some additional powers. Each state would continue to have equal representation regardless of population or geographical size. This was similar to the legislature under the Articles of Confederation. The more populous states thought the New Jersey plan was unfair because they did not think small and large states should have equal power in the proposed legislature. The convention rejected the New Jersey Plan and adopted the Connecticut Plan also known as the Great Compromise.

NONPARTISAN ELECTIONS

In a nonpartisan election, individuals competing for office have no official political party label although voters may know the political identification of the candidates. The two individuals with the most votes then have a runoff election to determine the winner. In this type of election two candidates from the same party may end up running against each other. There are relatively few nonpartisan elections in the United States. Most of these elections are for local offices.

OFFICE OF MANAGEMENT AND BUDGET (OMB)

The OMB is one of several instruments available to the president to exercise some control over the budgetary process. The OMB evaluates programs to try to ensure their relevance to the president's objectives. The office also judges the budgetary requests of the various agencies and departments. A major function of the OMB is to rationalize the entire budgetary process to try to make budget the president presents to Congress each year. When department and agency heads submit their budgetary requests to the president, he expects them to abide by OMB guidelines. The president needs to control the budgetary process to demonstrate his leadership, advance his policy priorities and to control spending. Members of Congress are, most of the time, primarily interested in reelection and therefore seek to satisfy demands made by constituents. They often seek to protect and promote programs regardless of costs if such programs contribute to the reelection process. For example, at times member of Congress support military systems opposed by the Pentagon. Members do so when the systems benefit the member's district by protecting jobs. Protecting jobs almost always helps reelection prospects. President Nixon reorganized the OMB in 1970 and made it part of the Executive Office of the President.

OLIGARCHY

Oligarchy generally refers to ruling elites that control the levers of power, political and economic. Factors such as wealth, heredity, skills, or royalty may determine the nature of the oligarchy. If heredity is the basis for the oligarchy then it is a closed oligarchy because there is only one way to enter the ruling class. An open oligarchy relies on skills and talents. An example of this is the fact that some American presidents came from relatively modest backgrounds without any of the advantages of wealth or family connections. Presidents Truman, Eisenhower, and Nixon came from modest backgrounds. Others such as Presidents Roosevelt, Kennedy, and Bush came from wealthy families and enjoyed all its benefits. The term oligarchy is sometimes associated with the concept of "ruling elites." Those who support elite theory claim it makes no difference whether the Republican Party or the Democratic Party rules America because the ruling elites have the same values regardless of party affiliation. They also point out that the Ivy League universities educate many individuals that become part of the ruling elite. Critics of elite theory argue that individuals in the ruling class have different values and support different policies. **It would be difficult to identify a policy that did not have both supporters and opponents. There may be elite groups in the Democratic and Republican parties but these groups must complete for popular support through the electoral system.**

ORIGINAL JURISDICTION

Original jurisdiction is the right of a court to be the first to hear a case. The Supreme Court, for example, has original jurisdiction in cases involving a conflict between the legislative and executive branches of government or a conflict between the states. Original jurisdiction is contained in Article III, section 2 of the Constitution.

If the Supreme Court hears a case based on original jurisdiction, the parties involved in the dispute cannot appeal the decision.

PLURALISM

Political pluralism is the ability of many diverse groups to influence public policies. Pluralism allegedly promotes moderation because no one group is able to dominate the decision making process therefore the need to make compromises. Pluralist theory is an alternative to elitist theory that claims relatively few people influence government decisions. Pluralism accepts the fact that elites influence government policies but there are many elites often in competition with each other. If some elite groups want the government to build more ballistic missiles for defense almost inevitably other elite groups will take the opposite position. Elites differ on policy positions and may have little influence on problems not associated with their expertise. In addition, elites must frequently appeal to a larger constituency to support the policy preferences of the elite group. Presidential elections illustrate the point because they reflect the values of different groups. Presidential candidates must appeal to many groups to put together enough votes to win the election. Candidates cannot rely on one or two voting groups for victory. Elites may be powerful and influential but they are not monolithic. Pluralism reflects the distribution of power in a political system.

PLURALITY VOTING

Plurality voting simply means an individual can win an election by obtaining the most votes even if that is not an absolute majority of fifty-one percent or more. If a Democratic candidate for office receives forty percent of the vote, a Republican Party candidate thirty percent, and an independent candidate thirty percent, the Democrat wins the election. Plurality voting helps maintain the two party systems in the United States because votes for a third party candidate generally hurts one of the two major parties. Third party candidates rarely win elections but they may help determine the winner. Plurality voting also applies to the Electoral College. In presidential elections the winning candidate in most states need only win more votes than his opponent to win all the electoral votes. Winning an absolute majority is not necessary.

POLICE POWERS

Police powers are powers states have based on the Tenth Amendment. States have an obligation to protect the health, morals, and safety of people living in the state. States may, for example, regulate drinking laws, motor vehicle inspections, and building codes. States may also determine qualifications for lawyers, doctors, and other professional groups.

POLITICAL ACTION COMMITTEES (PACs)

A Political Action Committee is a group of individuals supporting a political candidate or a political cause. Interest groups, labor unions, and corporations create PACS to help finance a candidate or a cause. By law, contributions of individuals to PACs may not exceed $5,000. In a landmark decision in 2010, Citizens United v Federal Election Commission, the Supreme Court ruled that the First Amendment prevented the government from limiting the amount of money corporations or unions could spend to help elect a candidate but restrictions to the candidates and political parties remained intact. The ruling enabled groups to organize Super PACS that could spend millions of dollars on advertising to help elect a candidate. As a result of the ruling, Super PACS became important and controversial actors in the electoral process. Although Super PACS can spend an unlimited amount of money to help elect a candidate they cannot coordinate their activities with the candidate running for office nor can they contribute money directly to the candidate or his political party. Critics claim that political operatives can easily skirt this restriction. They think it is absurd to believe there is no cooperation between the candidate and the Super PACS working for the candidate's election and spending huge sums of money. Super PACS may attack political opponents with negative ads without their candidate being held responsible for the attacks.

POLITICAL PARTIES: DEVELOPMENT

The founding fathers did not approve of political parties in part because they represented "factions" rather than the national interest. Despite their disapproval, individuals supporting similar policies morphed into political parties. Two major factions developed during the early days of the republic organized around the policies of Alexander Hamilton and his political opponent, Thomas Jefferson. Those supporting Hamilton organized the Federalist Party. Those supporting Jefferson organized the Democratic-Republicans. As a result of disagreements regarding the slave issue, the Federalist Party split into factions, lost its popular appeal, and morphed into the Whig Party in the 1820s. Subsequently, the slave issue destroyed the Whig Party. Whigs living in the north then created the Republican Party that emerged as the major opposition to the Democratic Party. Abraham Lincoln was the first president elected as a Republican. In 1860, he defeated Stephen Douglas the Democratic Party candidate.

The Democratic-Republican Party split in the 1820s. The faction led by Andrew Jackson became the Democratic Party. The two parties, Republican and Democratic, have remained the dominant parties ever since 1860. Third parties exist but ordinarily do not seriously challenge the two major parties. Third parties usually appeal to voters dissatisfied with the major parties and the policy choices they offer. Political party viability is largely determined by winning elections. In the United States, third parties rarely win elections in part because independents generally vote for one of the two major parties. Voters believe that voting for a third party is a wasted vote because third party candidates rarely win. Voters are not enthusiastic about going to the polls and voting for a candidate unlikely to win. Voters that dislike candidates of both political parties generally just do not vote.

POLITICAL PARTY IDENTIFICATION

Most voters identify with either the Republican Party or the Democratic Party. Identification may be strong, moderate, or weak. Party identification is less significant now than in the past. Many voters now split their ticket. They may vote for a Democrat running for a House seat and a Republican seeking a Senate seat. Party loyalty has declined over the years but some voters continue to identify with one party or the other. These voters make up the base of support for one party or the other. For the base of the party individual qualifications may be less important than a strong party identification. Now, more voters shift their party allegiance from one election to the next. In the past, voters tended to identify with their party for extended periods, sometimes a lifetime, and did not split their ticket. Now more voters rely on television and other media outlets to evaluate candidates rather than rely on party identification. Candidates for office are much more visible now than in the past.

POLITICAL PARTY PLATFORMS

Every four years the Republican and Democratic parties write a platform expressing what the party stands for and what it might do should it win the presidential election. The party platform will sometimes ignore or fudge controversial issues but will usually reveal important differences between the two parties. What goes into a party platform may generate considerable debate and controversy among party factions. This is usually the case if the campaign for the nomination has been competitive. In 1948, a number of southern delegates walked out of the Democratic Party convention because they opposed the civil rights plank of the party platform. They then convened their own convention and nominated Strom Thurmond for president. That same year, opponents of President Truman's policies towards Russia organized the Progressive Party and nominated Henry Wallace for president. Harry Truman managed to win reelection but by a slim margin. The 1968 Democratic Party convention erupted into violence because of policy differences regarding the Vietnam War. The party platform contained only one sentence dealing with the war. The Republicans won the presidential election. Contrary to what people think, the winning party does try to implement provisions of the party platform that best express the views and values of its members. Delegates attending the convention must approve the platform by a majority vote. Party leaders do their best to make the platform as appealing as possible. They want delegates to leave the convention dedicated to defeating the opposition party.

POLITICAL PARTIES: THIRD PARTIES

Although the Republican and Democratic political parties are the two major parties in the United States, third parties also play a political role. They do not organize the government nor do they usually have much influence in that process but they do serve several purposes. Third parties may decide to oppose a candidate of one of the major parties as a form of punishment. Conservative third party candidates may cause a Republican Party candidate to lose an election. Liberal party candidates can hurt the Democratic Party in the same way. Third parties may advocate an unpopular cause in the hope of eventually making the proposed policy more legitimate and popular. Some issues proposed by third parties that eventually became law include women's right to vote, child labor laws, and the forty hour work week. The Electoral College and the single member district with plurality voting makes it difficult for third parties to win elections, either national or local. The Electoral College works on a winner take all bases in forty-eight states. Two states, Nebraska and Maine distribute votes proportionally. Third parties may, however, win enough popular votes in a state to punish one of the two major candidates. Third party candidates helped defeat President H.W. Bush in 1992 and Al Gore in the 2000 presidential election. Plurality voting means a candidate can win an election despite receiving less than fifty-one percent of the votes. For example, a third party candidate might win thirty percent of the popular vote. The Republican Party candidate may also receive thirty percent of vote. The result would be a victory for the Democratic Party candidate although he receives only forty percent of the vote. Third parties may win the support of dissatisfied voters but the support is often fleeting. Third parties have difficulty attracting popular candidates and raising money because they do not win elections. They play a limited but at times an important role in the American political system.

POLITICAL QUESTION

The Supreme Court may refuse to hear a case if it involves a political question that should be resolved by a political process. An example of a political question may involve whether the president has the authority to send troops into battle without a congressional declaration of war. The Supreme Court usually avoids this issue by claiming it is a political question, not a constitutional question. Other political questions pertain to amending the Constitution and the power of Congress to impeach officials. These are nonjusticable political questions and therefore cannot be resolved in the courts.

POLITICAL TRIANGULATION

The term political triangulation is usually associated with former President Clinton and his effort to win a second term in the 1996 presidential election. Triangulation refers to the process of reconciling differences between the Republican and Democratic parties on a particular issue. Triangulation requires taking one solution offered by the Republican Party, a different solution offered by the Democratic Party and then meshing the two. By acting as a bridge between the parties, President Clinton could appear to be seeking bipartisan solutions, thereby rising above party politics. Analysts sometimes refer to political triangulation as the "third way." British Prime Minister Tony Blair was an advocate of the third way. The term is also associated with effort to combine the best of socialism and capitalism to form a third way. The expression "third way" has no precise meaning.

PORK BARREL LEGISLATION

Pork barrel legislation provides people in a congressional district or a state with certain benefits that will help an elected politician win political support. A benefit might take the form of a contract to erect some type of structure such as a bridge or a roadway that will create employment opportunities. Such projects may also improve safety factors on roadways. Other forms of pork may involve helping an organization by providing it with financial assistance. The politician will then use those benefits to help win reelection. Pork barrel legislation frequently translates into votes on election day. It is difficult to define what constitutes pork because members of Congress always claim the legislation they propose benefits many groups not just those living in the member's district. Pork-barrel legislation adds billions of dollars to the budget and is very difficult to control. Congressmen are not defeated because they support projects desired by the voters back home.

PRESIDENTIAL NOMINATING CAUCUS

Rather than a presidential primary election, several states use a caucus system to determine support for presidential nominees. The Iowa caucus is the best-known presidential caucus because it is the first state to engage in the nominating process. It receives a great deal of media coverage because it gives the American people and professional politicians an opportunity to judge the strength of presidential candidates if they are participating in the caucus. The winning candidate, particularly if it is an unexpected winner, receives national media attention. A victory also gives the winner momentum going into the New Hampshire primary election that usually takes place shortly after the Iowa caucus. The Iowa caucus is important because the media has made it so. This, despite the fact Iowa has only seven votes in the Electoral College and in many ways is not representative of the country as a whole. There are always national problems that may not be relevant to Iowa. A number of presidential candidates that have lost in Iowa or decided not to enter the caucus nevertheless have gone on to win the nomination. Since the 1970s, about half the candidates that won the Iowa caucus went on to win the nomination. Winning the Iowa caucus requires an extended organization and this is also a requirement for winning in other states.

PRIMARIES

PRIMARY ELECTIONS

Primary elections are a method for choosing political party candidates for state and national offices. The purpose of primaries is to give voters a choice in selecting their party nominees. There are many types of primaries. Political parties at the state level determine the type of primary they want but state governments and the national committees may impose certain rules and regulations.

To win the presidential nomination of either party, Republican or Democratic, candidates must enter and win a number of presidential primaries. Primaries determine the number of delegates committed to a particular candidate. In the past, political parties chose their nominee at presidential nominating conventions. Political leaders, sometimes referred to as bosses, often dominated the nominating process. After World War II, presidential primaries gradually became more important in the nominating process. In 1948, President Truman entered the New Hampshire primary and lost to Estes Kefauver. Truman then decided not to seek reelection. He allegedly did not base his decision on the outcome of New Hampshire but it must have had some influence on his decision. Kefauver won the primary but failed to win the nomination. In 1952, President Eisenhower upset Robert Taft in the New Hampshire primary and went on to win the Republican nomination and the election. Many observers expected a Taft victory in part because politicians often referred to him as "Mr. Republican." In 1964, Barry Goldwater was the surprise winner of a number of presidential primaries and succeeded in winning the Republican Party nomination. The experts expected a Rockefeller victory. In 1968, Hubert Humphrey won the Democratic presidential nomination despite opposition by many rank and file Democrats. Humphrey was the choice of the leaders of the Democratic Party but was not the choice of the rank and file who opposed the Vietnam War. During the primary process, many opponents of the Vietnam War supported Robert Kennedy. He won the California primary but there was not much celebrating. An assassin gunned him down. The assassination resulted in sharp divisions and disunity within the Democratic Party. Ever since 1972, the Democratic Party presidential nominee must win a majority of the delegates in the primary elections to win the nomination. Bosses no longer play the role they once did. The same is true for the Republican Party. Conventions now simply confirm the candidates winning the most primaries. There are no surprises at the convention and no genuine dark horses. Winning primary elections requires a great deal of money, multiple organizations, and a huge number of volunteer workers. A major criticism of presidential primaries is that they are not always representative of the rank and file of the party. The activists, always a minority, tend to dominate the presidential primary process.

PRIMARY ELECTIONS: CLOSED

In state primary elections, voters cast a ballot for their favorite candidate of their party. There are several types of primaries and each has advantages and disadvantages. Closed primary elections allow only party members to participate in the selection process. For example, in a Democratic Party primary only registered Democrats can vote. Rules pertaining to proof of party identification vary from state to state. In some states, you must have registered with the party before the date of the primary. In other states, you can declare your party identification on the day of the primary. Supporters of the closed primary system believe that only individuals that declare their party preference should have the right to help select the party nominee for a particular office.

PRIMARY ELECTIONS: CROSSOVER

Crossover primaries permit voters to cast their ballot in the primary of their choice regardless of party identification. A variation on this system is the practice of allowing voters to declare their party allegiance when they arrive at the polling station to vote. One problem with this type of primary is that individuals identified with one party may cast a ballot for the weakest candidate in the other party's primary. Their purpose is to help win the nomination of the candidate least likely to be an effective opponent in the general election. This practice does occur but it is difficult to know if it is effective.

PRIMARY ELECTIONS: FRONT-LOADING

Front-loading is the practice of states holding their presidential primaries as early as possible in an attempt to increase the importance of the state in the presidential nominating race. States, even large states, may have little influence selecting the party's candidate if the primary election takes place at the end of the year. If a candidate wins enough delegates in the early primaries to guarantee the nomination, voters have no incentive to go to the polls if their vote is without value. New Hampshire and Iowa, two small states that are not otherwise significant in the electoral process, are important because their presidential nominating contests occur early in the process. Both states are relatively insignificant in the presidential election because they have few electoral votes. Having a national primary rather than state primaries would eliminate the problem of front-loading but national primaries generate their own problems.

PRIMARY ELECTIONS: OPEN

See primaries: crossover

PRIMARY ELECTIONS: PROPORTIONAL VOTING

In primaries with proportional voting, the number of delegates awarded to the candidates is proportionate to the number of votes received. If a candidate wins thirty percent of the vote, he or she receives thirty percent of the delegates. The Democratic Party has more primaries with proportional voting than the Republican Party. Republicans usually prefer the winner takes all system of voting. Although the proportionate distribution of votes seems fairer than the winner take all system it may take longer to determine who will win the nomination. The winning candidate may not have enough time to heal party wounds. In some years, the parties may have some primaries that are winner takes all and some that permit proportional voting.

PRIMARY ELECTIONS: RUN OFF

In some states, the winning candidate in a primary election must receive fifty-one percent of the votes to win the election. Failure to do so necessitates a run-off election between the two candidates with the highest number of votes. This type of election generally occurs at the state level. When the Democratic Party dominated the south before the civil rights era, it dominated the electoral process. The primaries were much more important than the general elections because of the absence of a Republican Party candidate.

PRIMARY ELECTIONS: WINNER TAKES ALL

In winner takes all presidential primaries, the winner of the primary, regardless of size of the popular vote, wins all the delegates. The Republican Party usually prefers the winner takes all system of primaries. The Democratic Party prefers a system of proportional voting whereby the delegates a candidate wins is proportionate to the popular vote. States may change their voting preferences from one election to the next. The national committees of the two parties may require state parties to adopt a particular form of voting within a specific time period. For example, in the presidential primaries for the 2012 elections, the Republican National Committee ruled that all primaries held before April had to distribute votes on a proportionate basis rather than winner take all.

PRIMARIES: ADVANTAGES

Primaries allegedly provide voters with a number of advantages in the selection of presidential candidates. There are different types of primaries and they all have advantages and disadvantages. Primaries give people a voice in selecting the presidential candidate before voting in the general election. Participation in primaries came about in an effort to reform the nominating process the political bosses had dominated. Primaries enable candidates to test their popular appeal and their political message. If they have a political message that does not resonate with the people that will quickly become evident. The candidate can then repackage the message or discard it.

Unpopular candidates will have difficulty financing their campaigns because donors want to be sure they are backing a viable candidate. Raising money becomes one of the tests determining a candidate's viability particularly if there are many candidates. Finally, primaries enable candidates to determine issues voters believe are important. Candidates can enjoy a huge advantage if they select the right issues, those that connect with the voters. Candidates often struggle to determine the issues that excite or worry the voters. In the 2008 nominating conventions and the presidential election, Barak Obama emphasized the need for change. That message obviously resonated with the American people because of dissatisfaction with President George W. Bush and the Republicans in Congress.

PRIMARIES: DISADVANTAGES

Presidential primaries have several disadvantages. They extend the presidential selection process over a long period. By election day, many voters have heard more than they wish to know about the candidates. The media covers the candidates twenty-four hours a day, seven days a week. This happens throughout the primary process and then continues after each party has selected its presidential candidate. The media also covers family members and they, too, must be careful what they say and do because anything can become public. Some critics claim the long presidential election process, including the primaries, may discourage people from voting. The process now lasts two years or longer. There are no official dates for the length of the nominating process. Some hopeful candidates begin campaigning immediately after a presidential election. That means there could be four years of campaigning. Critics also point to the low voter turnout in many primary elections casting doubt about the democratic nature of the primary system. In some primaries, voter turnout is as low as twenty percent of the eligible voters. Primaries are financially very expensive thus preventing some potential candidates from entering the race. Those without an adequate financial base usually drop out of the race after one loss. Raising enough money to be viable in the early primaries means candidates must begin their quest for funds long before the primaries begin. Voters that participate in the primary system are usually the most partisan and this too may be a distorting factor. The winner of a primary may be the candidate with the most passionate support rather than one that more genuinely represents his party's principles.

PRIMARIES: PROPSED REFORMS

Advocates of reform of the primary system have put forward a number of proposals. One is to reduce the length of the primary season by having regional primaries on a rotating basis. The political parties would agree to divide the country into a number of regions. If, for example, the Western region voted first in one primary, another region would be the first to vote four years later. Regional primaries would obviously reduce the total number of primaries and some reformers think they might reduce costs. Some political leaders favor a national primary. They advocate having just one primary because that would reduce the length of the primary system and would compel candidates to emphasize issues that are important to the nation as a whole rather than a particular region or state. This, however, can be a disadvantage. Some voters may be more concerned about local or regional issues rather than national issues. Some issues are vitally important to a particular section of the country. Advocates that wish to reform the primary system must face the fact the country is geographically huge, has many sectional interests, and a diversified voting base. These factors contribute to the expense of the primary system as well as its length. Candidates must raise huge sums of money in part because they must establish local, state, and national organizations to support their campaign. Candidates often need a good deal of money just to win enough name recognition to receive media attention to get his or her message out to the public. All reform proposals have defects that mirror their advantages. There is no one primary system to satisfy all the different political constituencies. There is no such thing as a neutral primary. States prefer the type of primary that will advantage the state.

PRIOR RESTRAINT

Prior restraint is the ability of the government to prevent publication of material it wants to keep confidential. The government may also try to limit free speech by preventing someone from talking about a particular topic. Prior restraint is a form of censorship. The courts, particularly the Supreme Court, review prior restraint cases critically because the practice limits First Amendments freedoms. Governments sometimes try to prevent disclosure of information that may be embarrassing and politically harmful. A famous case involving prior restraint pertained to the Pentagon Papers. The papers demonstrated the fact the government consistently misinformed the American people about decisions regarding the Vietnam War. In 1971, the New York Times began publishing parts of the Pentagon Papers. The Nixon administration tried to prevent publication alleging it would harm America's national security. The case went to the Supreme Court and it ruled against Nixon. Preventing publication of the papers was an example of prior restraint and therefore unconstitutional.

PROSPECTIVE VOTING

Prospective voting occurs when a voter casts a ballot for a candidate based on positive expectations about the future. In the 1952 presidential election, many voters cast a ballot for Dwight Eisenhower because of his promise to end the Korean War. Richard Nixon won the 1968 election because of his promise to end the Vietnam War. It is often difficult to differentiate between prospective and retrospective voting. In both types of elections, voters may be demonstrating their displeasure with past policies and their optimism about the future. The two often go hand in hand.

REALIGNING ELECTION

See critical elections

REAPPORTIONMENT AND REDISTRICTING

Reapportionment occurs every ten years after the census determines the population of the country and the distribution of population among the states. Reapportionment determines the number of representatives a state is entitled to in the House of Representatives as a result of population changes since the previous census. Reapportionment can affect the influence of states, sections of the country, and political parties. In 1964, California replaced New York as the most populous state and therefore was entitled to more seats in the House of Representatives and more votes in the Electoral College. It now has fifty-three representatives in the House and fifty-five electoral votes. It thus plays an important role in the national legislative process and presidential elections. Despite the size of the population, each state is automatically entitled to one representative. Wyoming has two senators but only one member of the House of Representatives. Reapportionment can shift the power in Congress from one party to another and the shift may last ten years, until the next census. After reapportionment, state legislatures usually redraw congressional districts to reflect shifts in population from one part of the state to another. They may have to add or subtract districts if the population of the state has increased or decreased. This is the redistricting process. State legislatures try to redraw district boundaries in a way that favors the political party dominating the legislature. Redistricting may change the size of districts within the state to reflect changes in the population since the last census. The total membership of the House of Representatives is four hundred and thirty five. The number does not automatically change because of an increase in the population. Periodically, Congress will decide to increase the size of the House based on the increase in the country's population. When the Congress first met in 1789, the House had sixty-five members. The House has had four hundred and thirty five members since 1911. The United States then had a population of less than one hundred million. It now has a population of more than three hundred million but still has only four hundred and thirty five members.

RECONSTRUCTION ERA

The Reconstruction era followed the civil war and lasted from 1865 to 1877. The national government appointed individuals, derisively called Carpetbaggers, to govern the defeated southern states. They established conditions the southern states had to meet before they could regain their political independence. During this period, the Democratic Party became the dominant party in the south. Republican candidates could not win elections because they were associated with the end of slavery, the Civil War, and the reconstruction era. After the reconstruction era, state governments, controlled by the Democratic Party, passed Jim Crow laws to keeps blacks subservient and to guarantee continued white dominance. The Ku Klux Klan became a dominant force in the South and often resorted to violent methods to keep blacks from winning any rights or gaining any power. The southern states became a solid base for the Democratic Party until the passage of civil rights legislation in the 1960s.

RED AND BLUE STATES

The expression red and blue states was first used in the 2000 presidential election. The colors have no significance other than as an identifying mark. The red states are Republican. The blue states are democratic. The colors are a useful device when watching television. They enable the viewer to easily identify Republican or Democratic states.

REDISTRICTING

Redistricting is the policy of state legislatures to redraw geographical political districts every ten years following the decennial census. The party controlling the state legislature usually tries to redraw voting district boundaries to help their members win elections. Redistricting can result in making a congressional seat "safe" to guarantee victory. This may lead to more partisanship because challenges to the incumbent occur in the primary rather than the general election. Challengers to incumbents frequently come from the left wing of the Democratic Party or the right wing of the Republican Party. Redistricting is sometimes confused with reapportionment but the two are distinct. Reapportionment highlights the importance of the decennial census because it determines how many representatives the state is entitled to in the House of Representatives. How districts are redrawn helps determine which of the two parties, the Republicans or Democrats, will be dominant in the state. This process also impacts Congress. A state dominated by one political party has a better chance to elect members to Congress than does the minority party.

171

REPUBLICAN PARTY

The Republican Party dates back to 1854 when the Whig Party was in decline. Many supporters of the Whig party that lived in the north joined the Republican Party. In 1860, Abraham Lincoln was the first Republican elected president. Although people who identify with the Republican Party have a diversity of views, most share certain principles including limited government, fiscal conservatism, low taxes, and a strong national defense. Republicans are more conservative than Democrats. Republicans generally support equality of opportunity but not equality of results. Despite a core set of principles, parties do at times undergo fundamental changes. After World War I, many Republican leaders identified with isolationist foreign policies but this changed with the election of Dwight Eisenhower in 1952. He was the first Republican elected president since 1928. He was a popular national leader because of his military role during World War II. His presidency helped modernize the Republican Party. He convinced many Republicans to accept many of the New Deal reforms initiated by President Roosevelt after 1932. Eisenhower easily won reelection in 1956. After Eisenhower, the most popular Republican was Ronald Reagan. He won the 1980 presidential election and was reelected in 1984. In that election he won forty nine of the fifty states. Although he was a conservative Republican, he was also willing to work with Democrats in Congress when he thought it was in the national interest to do so.

RESERVED POWERS

The American Constitution distributes power between national and state governments in three ways: delegated, reserved, and concurrent. Reserved powers are powers exercised by state governments. Examples of reserved powers include regulation of intrastate trade, establishing local governments, and redistricting. States also have police powers. States use these powers to protect the welfare and safety of people. Examples are regulations dealing with the handling of food, preserving public order, and fire prevention.

RETAIL POLITICS

Retail politics is the process whereby politicians meet small groups of people to win their support. Politicians will meet in such places as private homes, well-known restaurants, or town halls. He or she will try to shake hands and chat with as many voters as possible. One of the best examples of retail politics is the New Hampshire presidential primary. Presidential candidates usually make many trips to the state to meet with as many people as possible. Retail politics is less effective in large states such as New York or California but politicians may still want to have face-to-face contacts with particular groups of voters in those states. Some politicians are much better at retail politics than others because they appear to be comfortable kissing babies, tasting ethnic foods, and mingling with small groups of people. Politicians, however comfortable they are with retail politics, now stick to a safe script. They know whatever they say could be picked up by the national media and misinterpreted. Politicians try to avoid spontaneous comments that might get them into trouble.

RETROROSPECTIVE VOTING

Retrospective voting occurs when an individual votes for a candidate based on his or her past actions in office. People may vote to reelect or defeat a president because they approve or disapprove of his policies during his first term. Critics sometimes compare retrospective voting with prospective voting.

RINO

RINO refers to individuals who are Republican in Name Only. It is a pejorative term used to describe Republicans who are not sufficiently conservative or are willing to cooperate with Democrats if it is in the national interest to do so. The term RINO also reflects divisions within the Republican Party between the conservative and more moderate or liberal wings.

RULE OF FOUR

Four Supreme Court judges must agree to hear a case before it is placed on the Court calendar. Each year the Court receives thousands of petitions but agrees to hear approximately one hundred cases. The judges agree to hear those cases they believe are the most important.

SECULAR REALIGNMENT

Secular realignment is the process by which voters switch their allegiance from one political party to another over a prolonged period. This contrasts with a realigning election that occurs during one election cycle. Critics do not use the two terms, secular and realignment, much anymore. Many voters are no longer loyal to one party or another for a prolonged period.

SELECT COMMITTEE (TEMPORARY COMMITTEE)

Either house of Congress may create a select committee, also known as a temporary committee, to deal with a specific topic or problem. Congress has created select committees to deal with problems related to such things as aging, energy resources, and nutrition. Congress dissolves select committees after they comple their tasks.

SENATE LEADERSHIP

The majority party in the Senate chooses the leader of the Senate. As the leader, he must try to keep his party unified to promote policies the party favors. He has many housekeeping chores to keep the Senate functioning and he must be alert to the needs of members of his party. His relationship to the Speaker of the House and the president depends on such things as whether the three are in the same or different political parties.

SENATORIAL COURTESY

Senatorial courtesy is the custom whereby the president, when selecting individuals to fill federal vacancies including federal marshals, federal district court judges, and other federal vacancies, consults the Senator representing that state if both belong to the same political party. Sometimes Senators will suggest individuals the president might consider nominating. This custom is not required by the Constitution. Should the president ignore a request from a Senator, the Senate might refuse to hold hearings for approving the president's appointment. The refusal is a courtesy the Senate grants to all its members. The practice continues because all members are potential beneficiaries.

SEPTEMBER 11

On September 11, 2001, terrorist members of al-Qaeda, hijacked four passenger planes to carry out a terrorist attack against the United

States. Two planes crashed into the World Trade Towers in New York City. Both buildings collapsed trapping many people in the burning buildings. A third plane crashed into the Pentagon. Passengers took control of a fourth plane and crashed it into open fields near Shanksville, Pa. The terrorists flying that plane were apparently headed for the White House. The various attacks killed approximately 3,000 people. Many more were injured including individuals that took part in the rescue operations. Some of the injured subsequently died. One month after the attacks, the United States invaded Afghanistan to eliminate the al-Qaeda threat. In 2003, American military forces invaded Iraq despite the fact there was no good evidence that Iraq was implicated in the 9/11 attacks. As a result of 9/11 the United States launched a global counter-terrorism offensive.

SIGNING STATEMENTS

Signing statements are statements made by the president when he signs a legislative bill. His statement generally gives his opinion about the meaning of legislation and how he intends to enforce it. The president sometimes issues a statement because he wants to make public how he interprets the legislation. His interpretation may differ from what legislators had in mind when they passed the legislation. The president may also indicate that he does not plan to implement provisions of the legislation. Signing statements are controversial. Critics claim the president does not have the right to alter legislation by deciding what he will or will not implement. His interpretation may undermine the intent of the legislation. Some critics claim that signing statements are similar to the line item veto that the Supreme Court has ruled to be unconstitutional. When he was running for president, Barak Obama criticized President George W. Bush for his many signing statements. Once in office, President Obama continued the practice of issuing signing statements that he once deplored.

SINGLE MEMBER DISTRICTS

A single member district is an electoral district that elects just one individual. This is in contrast to a multi-member district. Single member districts helps to maintain the two political party system. This type of district allegedly helps promote a closer relationship between the voters and the elected official. If a constituent has a problem or wants to promote a particular policy or idea, he or she can go directly to the one elected official that represents the constituent's district.

SOCIAL CONTRACT THEORY

Social contract theory holds that people enter into a contract when they and their leaders agree to form a government. Prominent social contract theorists include John Locke, Thomas Hobbes, and Jacques Rousseau. Hobbes believed that life in a state of nature is nasty and brutish. He believed people are rational and therefore willingly give up their rights in return for law and order. The primary function of every government is the maintenance of order. The social contract obligates the government to carry out this function. John Locke had a profound influence on delegates attending the Constitutional Convention. He believed people and their leaders entered into a contract that limited the power of government and protected the rights of people. If government violates the social contract, people have the right to rebel. The idea of a contract limits the powers of the government and protects people's rights and freedoms. A democratic social contract theory also implies the right of people to rebel against the government if it violates the contract by denying people their rights and freedoms. The Constitution is an example of a social contract. The separation of powers and the system of checks and balances are a part of a social contract. The social contract in America protects the basic rights of people and delegates enough power to government to carry out it functions.

SOCIALIZATION PROCESS: AGENTS OF

The primary agents of the socialization process are the family, schools, and the media. The three continue to be significant in passing along values, beliefs, and attitudes, from one generation to another. There are now many more agents of the socialization process than in the past. In the past, if a family participated in the electoral process, most members of the family voted the same way. This is no longer necessarily so. Today, a husband and wife might both be employed and because of their exposure to different viewpoints, may very well have different and contradictory political outlooks. Today, there are multiple media outlets expressing very different opinions about international, national, and local issues. The media today is much more fractured than in the past. Children, in addition to learning from their parents, are now exposed to much more information from many different sources. Numerous media outlets intentionally direct their messages to children. The values children acquire are now often in conflict with those the parents might want to pass along.

SPEAKER OF THE HOUSE

The Speaker of the House is always the leader of the majority party who has ordinarily been in Congress for a number of years. The Speaker is second in line to become president if he dies or is unable to perform his duties. The power of the Speaker depends on many factors including leadership abilities, the size of the majority in the House, and his or her relationship with the president. In the past, Speakers had almost dictatorial power but this is no longer true. The House of Representatives has become much more democratic. The Speaker must always remain attuned to the wishes of his constituents that elected him to Congress.

SPLIT TICKET VOTING

Split ticket voting is the practice of voting for members of both political parties rather than vote for all candidates from one party. An example would be a voter casting a ballot for a Republican member of Congress and the presidential candidate of the Democratic Party. Split ticket voting has become popular in the United States although it contributes to the difficulty of holding parties responsible for what they do. Voters like to vote for candidates from both parties because they think such a practice promotes bipartisanship but there is not much evidence supporting this thesis. Some observers describe split ticket voting as another aspect of the system of checks and balances.

STANDING COMMITTEE

Standing committees are the permanent committees in the House and Senate. They do most of the important work on legislative bills before they go to the floor. The Senate has sixteen standing committees; the House has twenty three. Committee chairs are members of the majority party. Both the majority and minority members have staff personnel that do much of the legislative work such as research, coordinating with members of other committees, and consulting with important constituent groups. Members often remain on standing committees for long periods and thus acquire expertise on subjects under the committee's jurisdiction. Remaining on a committee also enables members to establish seniority. Expertise and seniority are both a source of power in Congress.

STATE OF THE UNION

Every year the president addresses a joint session of Congress to report on the "State of the Union." He directs his address to three audiences: the world, the nation, and the Congress. A part of his address always deals with foreign policy issues. Leaders around the world pay careful attention to the address. It enables them to get a better understanding of American goals and values. His ability to win public approval for his policies is important because it is a major source of presidential power, both foreign and domestic. The legislative part of the president's address enables him to better control the legislative agenda by explaining his priorities and their importance. The Constitution requires the president to evaluate the state of the union but it says nothing about how to deliver the message. There is no constitutional requirement that the president actually appear before Congress. President Washington appeared before a joint session of Congress to deliver the address. Rather than appear in person, Thomas Jefferson sent a letter to Congress on the State of the Union. Presidents followed that precedent until 1913 when President Wilson appeared before a joint session of Congress to deliver the address. In 1947, President Truman was the first president to have the speech televised. President Johnson was the first president to deliver the State of the Union Address in the evening. The State of the Union address has become an important media event ever since President Truman first televised the address in 1947. There are times when the State of the Union address resembles a political rally. Members of the president's party stand up and applaud at every opportunity while members of the opposition usually just sit in silence.

SUPER TUESDAY

Super Tuesday is the day most states hold their presidential primary elections. It usually takes place in February or March. The results of Super Tuesday can significantly influence the ultimate choice of the party if one candidate does particularly well by winning in many states and/or winning the big states. In 2008, twenty-two states held primaries on Super Tuesday. Barak Obama won most of the delegates but only a few more than Hillary Clinton. One criticism of Super Tuesday is that it favors the candidates with the most money and the best organization. Another criticism is the fact the candidates spend little time in the smaller states with the fewest delegates. Super Tuesday now has some of the attributes of a national primary but candidates still try to do well in the early primaries in the hope this will give them greater momentum leading to Super Tuesday. Gaining momentum requires candidates to begin campaigning early in the presidential election cycle. Early campaigning requires they spend more time raising funds to finance the campaign.

SUPREMACY CLAUSE

Article VI paragraph 2, of the Constitution declares the laws passed by Congress to be the supreme law of the land. State laws or courts cannot nullify or ignore such laws. The supremacy clause corrected one of the defects in the Articles of Confederation. An early test of the supremacy clause came in 1819. The national government created a national bank. Maryland decided it wanted to tax the bank. This clash of powers produced a major constitutional issue that was resolved by the Supreme Court's decision McCullough v. Maryland 1819. The Court invoked the supremacy clause and ruled that Maryland could not tax the bank because taxation implies the ability to control. The tax would have given Maryland the right to control a power of the national government. In voting with the majority, Chief Justice John Marshall said the power to tax is the power to destroy. Congress and the courts have interpreted the supremacy clause to enlarge the powers of the national government. One of the goals at the Constitutional Convention was to grant the national government sufficient powers to deal effectively with problems it was unable to cope with under the Articles of Confederation. The distribution of power between the national and state governments is a never ending problem because of changing circumstances.

SUPREME COURT: JUDICIAL DECISION MAKING

Many factors influence judicial decision-making including relevant law, previous cases, political ideology, legal philosophies, and the prevailing political climate. Interpreting the law is a dynamic process and this is one reason why confirmation hearings may be contentious. Supreme Court rulings can have significant consequences. The 1857 Dred Scott decision contributed to the outbreak of the Civil War in 1861. Supreme Court decisions dealing with economic issues during President Roosevelt's first term had disastrous consequences on the government's ability to deal with the effects of the 1929 economic crash. Judges do not always vote as expected nor is their previous experience necessarily a good predictor. Judges may change their opinions because of new circumstances, the influence of other judges, or a different way of thinking about a problem. Judicial precedents are significant but not binding. There were many judicial precedents supporting segregation policies but the 1954 Brown v. Board of Education ruling eliminated many of them. Critics often categorize judges as being liberal or conservative or leaning in one direction or the other. Although judges may claim to be objective, the fact is there is almost always an ideological divide between liberal and conservative judges. Most judges consistently align with one ideology or the other.

SWING STATES

In presidential elections, some states consistently vote for one of the two major parties, Republican or Democratic. New York and California usually cast their ballots for the Democratic Party presidential candidate. Mississippi and Texas consistently support the Republican Party. Swing states are those that do not consistently vote for one party or the other. The important swing states in presidential elections are those with a substantial number of Electoral College votes. Some states remain swing states for many elections but others may be relevant to a particular election. Ohio is a classic example of a swing state but also important is the fact that it often casts its votes for the winning candidate in the presidential race. It has voted for the winning candidate in the last twelve presidential elections. This record endows Ohio with more importance than just being a swing state. A presidential candidate can win the election by getting a majority of votes in the eleven states with the most electoral votes. In the past, voters in Florida and Virginia usually cast their ballots for the Republican Party candidates but they now seem to be moving into the swing state category. Presidential candidates tend to spend less time and money in states they do not expect to win. They may do the same in states where they are confident of victory. They spend more time and money in the swing states because they determine the winner in presidential elections.

SYMBOLIC SPEECH

Symbolic speech is the expression of ideas without using words. An example of symbolic speech would be wearing a patch of some sort on clothing that expresses a political thought. Burning the American flag is considered symbolic speech. The Supreme Court has ruled that the First Amendment protects symbolic speech although there are exceptions. Public school officials may prohibit students from wearing symbols on their clothing if they would cause disturbances in the school.

TERM LIMITS: CONGRESS

Some states have attempted to limit the number of terms an individual may serve in Congress. Supporters of term limits believe office holders become entrenched in office because of the difficulty of ousting an incumbent. The reelection rate for incumbents in Congress is about ninety percent. Effectively challenging incumbents is difficult because of the many advantages they enjoy including name recognition and fund raising. Proponents of term limits believe limiting the number of years an individual may serve in Congress would be an effective remedy to deal with the entrenchment problem. They also believe that if there is a limit applied to the president, limits should be applied to members of Congress. In 1995, the Supreme Court ruled that state legislation limiting the number of terms an individual could serve in Congress was unconstitutional.

TERM LIMITS: PRESIDENT

Term limits is the policy of limiting the number of years one may serve in an elective office. When the founding fathers wrote the

Constitution, they placed no limits on the number of terms a president or a member of congress could serve. After serving two terms, President Washington decided, despite his popularity, not to seek a third term. He could have easily won a third term if he decided to run. Washington knew that many American political leaders opposed the idea of an individual remaining in office too long. The colonial experience reinforced the idea that people in power for too long a period often abused their power. Washington's decision not to seek a third term created an important precedent that remained in effect until World War II when President Roosevelt decided on a third and then a fourth term. President Roosevelt was elected in 1932 and reelected in 1936. At the end of his second term, he remained popular and continued to have the confidence of the American people. This was important because the United States had not yet recovered from the 1929 crash. In 1939, war broke out in Europe that soon engulfed the entire region. China and Japan were also at war. America's relations with Japan were increasingly hostile in part because Japan was allied with Italy and Germany. Roosevelt decided to run for a third term because of continued economic problems combined with the increasingly hostile global environment. He won the 1940 election with about 55% of the popular vote. He ran again in 1944 despite his failing health. In April 1945, five months after his election victory, he died. At time of his death, Roosevelt was seriously ill and had been for some time. Critics opposed some decisions he made towards the end of the war particularly at the 1945 Yalta conference. There was speculation that Roosevelt was too ill to effectively deal with the problems on the agenda of the Yalta meeting. In 1951, the states ratified the Twenty-second amendment limiting the president to two terms. The amendment returned the country to the precedent established by George Washington.

THINK TANKS

Think tanks are organizations that analyze problems, propose solutions to problems, or simply spell out policy alternatives. They do much of their work for government agencies, political parties and policy makers. Think Tanks may be liberal or conservative or nonpartisan. They deal with a broad range of issues including foreign policy, economic, social, technological, or other types of issues. Individuals working as policy makers, when their party is in power, will sometimes join a Think Tank when their party is out of power. A major criticism of Think Tanks is they have deepened the ideological divide that seems to separate the two major political parties making it more difficult for political leaders to reach compromise solutions.

UNITARY GOVERNMENT

The distribution of power in a nation state may take three forms: unitary, federal, or confederal. A government controlling most levers of power characterizes a unitary state. The national government may create regional and local government offices but may also abolish them. Great Britain has a unitary form of government. This form of government is not suitable for a democratic country with a large geographical area to govern. Although a nation may have a unitary form of government and be democratic, as is the case in Great Britain, nondemocratic governments usually have a unitary form of government.

VETO POWER: PRESIDENT

The Constitution grants the president the right to veto legislation approved by Congress. After Congress passes a bill, the president must sign or veto it within ten days unless Congress adjoins and is not in session. In that case, failing to sign a bill in effect becomes a presidential veto. The president puts the bill in his pocket (hence the term pocket veto) without signing it. The president may also veto legislation with a message explaining the reason for his decision. Congress may override the veto with a two-thirds vote in both houses. The president can influence legislation by simply indicating he intends to veto a bill if it contains provisions he opposes.

VICE PRESIDENT

The president largely determines the functions of the Vice President. His only constitutional function is as President of the Senate. With the exception of Lyndon Johnson, every Vice President since 1952 has performed many important political tasks. Lyndon Johnson did not have a close relationship with President Kennedy. Ever since President Eisenhower, every Vice President except for two, has tried to win his party's nomination for president or has won the nomination and then tried to win the presidential election. In 1973, Vice President Spiro Agnew did not try to win the presidential nomination because he had to resign as Vice President because of a corruption scandal. Law enforcement officials accused Agnew of taking bribes, tax fraud, and bribery. He made a deal with the prosecution and agreed to resign. Dick Cheney, who served as Vice President to President George W. Bush, was old and ill at the end of Bush's second term.

VIRGINIA PLAN

James Madison was the author of the Virginia Plan. It called for a two house national legislature. Voters would determine the composition of the lower house. Members of the lower house would then elect members of a second chamber based on nominations submitted by the states. Large states supported the Virginia Plan, small states opposed it. Under the Articles of Confederation all states were equal. They each had one vote regardless of population or geographical size. The Virginia Plan called for the creation of three branches of government and a system of checks and balances. The conflict between those supporting the New Jersey Plan and those supporting the Virginia Plan led to the Connecticut Plan also called the Great Compromise. The Virginia Plan was important because it framed the debate about the political structure needed to govern the country. The Virginia Plan was obviously incompatible with a confederal form of government. When Madison's plan became the focus of debate, many delegates quickly realized that his plan, or some version of it, meant scrapping the Articles of Confederation. Madison's plan shaped the agenda of the convention.

VOTING: PARTY IDENTIFICATION

Voters that identify strongly with a political party are more likely to vote than those with no party or a weak party affiliation. The fact is however, that party identification has declined over the years. More and more people do not identify with either political party, the Republicans or the Democrats for long periods. Voters and potential voters now often rely on television for political cues. They may rely on individuals such as Jay Leno, or Jon Stewart or Stephen Colbert. They are also more likely to rely on messages they receive from particular shows such as Saturday Night Live or The O'Reilly Factor. Issues and personality are often more important voting variables than party identification. Those individuals that continue to identify with one political party or another do so with much less fervor. Another factor that has weakened party identification is the growing propensity of voters to split their vote. Voters seem to like the idea of divided government—one party controlling the White House, the other controlling Congress. Although party identification has declined, voters continue to vote for one of the two major parties.

VOTING: PRESIDENTIAL ELECTIONS

Many Americans frequently fail to exercise their right to vote. Experts in voting behavior generally distinguish between two groups of potential voters, the adult population and those eligible to vote. Some adults, for a variety of reasons, are not eligible to vote, others just do not register. Most voting participation occurs every four years in the presidential election. Voting turnout in presidential elections usually ranges between fifty and sixty percent of the voting age population. There are many reasons why people do not vote in addition to qualifications. Some non-voters dislike both the Republican and Democratic parties and dislike the candidates of one or both political parties. Some reform advocates would like voting to take place on Sunday. They believe that would increase the voting turnout because people have more leisure time on Sunday. Other advocates would like to have voters automatically registered to increase the number of eligible voters. In some countries, the government is responsible for registering voters. Nine states in the United States have automatic registration and voting turnout in those states is generally higher than in other states. Some studies suggest that if people who do not vote did vote the outcome would be about the same. Non-voters simply reflect the beliefs and values of those who do vote.

VOTING BEHAVIOR

It is often difficult to know exactly why people vote as they do unless there is an obvious issue that captures the national mood. Two such issues are war and economics. There is no doubt the election of

Eisenhower in 1952 and Nixon in 1968 was in part due to the Korean and Vietnam wars. Although the approval rating for President Bush H.W. was quite high after the Gulf War in 1992 he lost his reelection bid primarily because of the weak economy. Those that voted for Bill Clinton that year did not necessarily understand his economic policies but they had confidence he would do better than President George W. W. Bush. Economic conditions also helped Barak Obama win the 2008 presidential election. He emphasized the need for change and that proved to be very appealing despite the fact it never was clear what specific changes he had in mind. Presidential election outcomes are often an expression of a mood rather than an endorsement of a specific policy. Voters may cast their ballot because they like or dislike a particular candidate. The effective use of the media can be a powerful force in shaping public opinion. In the past, party identification often determined voting behavior. Observers often ranked voters on the basis of their strong, medium, or weak commitment to a particular party. Strong identifiers almost always voted for the candidate of their party. Party identification is no longer as strong as it once was. Voters now often shift their loyalty from one party to the other depending on issues and personality.

WATERGATE SCANDAL

The Watergate scandal refers to a series of illegal activities carried out by individuals working to reelect President Nixon in 1972. He enjoyed an overwhelming victory by winning in forty-nine of fifty states. It was a great victory. In 1974, because of his involvement in the Watergate scandal he decided to retire rather than face impeachment charges. **Individuals working to reelect President Nixon in 1972 decided to break into the Democratic National Committee headquarters located in the Watergate hotel.** They apparently hoped to find information they could use against the Democratic

Party nominee, George McGovern. During the Senate investigation of the Watergate affair, members learned that the White House had a recording system to record conversations. These recordings clearly revealed Nixon's involvement in the cover up. It was also apparent he lied to members of his own party and repeatedly lied when questioned about Watergate events. Nixon knew he would have to resign when he learned that many Republicans supported his impeachment. More than thirty people did jail time because of their involvement in the Watergate scandal. In 1976, Democrats won control of both houses of Congress and the presidency. The irony of the Watergate scandal is the fact that Nixon could have easily won the election without resorting to the tactics that led to his resignation.

WAVE ELECTIONS

A wave election occurs when a political party wins a substantial number of electoral contests. There is no precise number to determine whether a wave election has occurred although some policy makers believe a loss of twenty congressional seats by a party constitutes a wave. A wave election might include one or both houses of Congress, gubernatorial, and state legislative elections. Wave elections occurred in 2006, 2008, and 2010. In 2008, the Democratic Party won control of the presidency, both houses of Congress, and numerous gubernatorial elections. In 2010, Republicans won control of the House, increased their numbers in the Senate, won most gubernatorial races, and increased their control of state legislatures. Before the election, Democrats controlled twenty six governorships, the Republicans twenty four. After the election, Republicans controlled twenty nine governorships, a gain of seven. A wave election generally indicates dissatisfaction with the incumbents. The fact that wave elections are not all that unusual in part reflects the fact that voters are frequently dissatisfied with incumbents regardless of what party controls the institution.

WAYS AND MEANS COMMITTEE

The Ways and Means Committee (Committee on Ways and Means) is one of the most important and powerful committees in the House of Representatives. It writes tax legislation and bills affecting many entitlement programs such as Social Security. It also deals with revenue raising measures, unemployment benefits, and trade legislation. Members of the Ways and Means Committee may not serve on any other committee. The size of the committee varies but usually has about forty members. Members of Congress are eager to serve on the committee because of its control over revenue. Committee members can effectively serve constituents by inserting tax legislation language that benefits groups back home or anywhere in the country. Business and other organizations such as charities are always interested in tax legislation that influences their well-being. Tax policies impact all Americans.

WELFARE STATE

In the United States, the inauguration of the welfare state is associated with the New Deal of President Roosevelt after his 1932 election. Numerous entitlement programs characterize the welfare state. The purpose of these programs is to provide a safety net to allow people to better cope with economic and social hardships. Welfare state policies include such things as minimum wage laws, unemployment insurance, workman's compensation, food stamps, and social security benefits. In the United States, the scope of welfare state benefits is often a contentious issue dividing Republicans and Democrats. Many of these programs become more expensive with the passing of time due to demographic changes. An increase in the number of people entitled to benefits plus the fact that people are living longer contributes to the costs of the welfare state. Curbing costs by reducing or eliminating benefits is difficult to do because of the electoral process. Voters do not elect politicians that promise to cut or reduce benefits if they are elected. Congress continues to fund programs the country can no longer afford and the result is substantial budget deficits that then create other economic and fiscal problems. This problem is present at the national and other levels of government. Deficits have an impact on the sustainability of other government programs. The problem of government costs is compounded by changes in the in the composition of the population. As the population ages and people live longer, government programs benefiting that segment of the population become more expensive. Many democracies are facing the same problems. The benefits of the welfare state are not necessarily limited to those that are needy or living in poverty. People who are economically well off also benefit from welfare state policies. To help curb costs, some policy makers advocate a means test to determine eligibility for benefits but such tests are not popular. Both state and the national government fund some welfare policies.

WHIG PARTY

In 1834, opponents of President Jackson organized the Whig Party. Whigs believed that President Jackson behaved more like a monarch than the leader of a democratic country. Henry Clay and Daniel Webster were prominent members of the party. It won the presidential election in 1840 and 1848. In one sense, the Whig Party adopted some of the policies associated with the Federalists before their demise after the 1800 election. Slavery was the divisive issue that split the Whig Party. Whigs in the north opposed slavery and eventually joined the Republican Party. At one point, Abraham Lincoln was a Whig. Whigs located in the South supported slavery and joined the Democratic Party. The Whig Party disappeared with the outbreak of the Civil War.

WHITE HOUSE CHIEF OF STAFF

In some respects, the most important individual managing White House affairs is the president's chief of staff. He helps manage the day-to-day affairs. The president may also rely on his chief of staff for advice on political and policy questions. One of his most important functions is to anticipate problems that might cause the president embarrassment. The chief of staff must deal with many important advisors and therefore needs a good deal of diplomatic skill if he is to serve the president effectively.

YELLOW DOG DEMOCRAT

The term Yellow Dog Democrat is no longer used. Southerners used the expression in the past to describe southern Democrats who would always vote for a Democrat, even if the Democrat was a dog. The southern antagonism towards the Republican Party was a heritage of the Civil War

CONSTITUTIONAL CONVENTION FACTS

1. Delegates at the 1786 Annapolis Convention suggested convening a convention to revise the Articles of Confederation
2. The Constitutional Convention met in Philadelphia from May to September 1789
3. The Constitutional Convention met to amend the Articles of Confederation, not to write a constitution
4. Fifty-five delegates attended the convention
5. Rhode Island did not send any delegates to the Convention
6. Delegates agreed to conduct deliberations in secret

7. John Adams, Thomas Jefferson, and Patrick Henry did not attend the convention

8. James Madison kept a record of the proceedings and is considered the father of the Constitution

9. Delegates elected George Washington to serve as president of the Constitutional Convention

10. The Bill of Rights was not a part of the original Constitution but was proposed to help ensure its ratification

11. Thirty nine of the fifty-five delegates signed the Constitution

12. Nine states had to ratify the Constitution before it became operative but it was essential that the large states also ratify it

13. The ninth state, New Hampshire, ratified the Constitution in 1788

14. Virginia, New York, and North Carolina, ratified the Constitution in 1789

15. Rhode Island withheld ratification until 1790

WARS IN AMERICAN HISTORY

REVOLUTIONARY WAR

The American War of Independence, 1775 to 1783, had many causes including taxation, representation, trade, boycotts, the billeting of British soldiers, and the attitude of the King George III. Fighting began in 1775 but it was not until a year later that the colonists decided they wanted to be independent. In 1776, the Continental Congress completed the Declaration of Independence. The Enlightenment and individuals such as John Locke influenced the decision to seek independence. Locke was an advocate of Social Contract theory. He believed that a social contract connected people to their government. If governments violated the contract, subjects had the right to rebel. The French government encouraged the revolution and supplied the colonists with needed resources before and after France officially declared war against Great Britain in 1778. The British were also at war with Spain and the Dutch Republic. The fact that Britain had three major adversaries besides the colonies helped the colonial cause. Geography also aided the colonists. The thirteen states covered a great deal of territory. The colonial forces could always retreat and regroup. They could win the war by not being defeated. This is similar to what we now call a guerrilla war. Transporting troops and equipment from Great Britain to the rebellious colonies was expensive and time consuming. George Washington led the American military effort. As a result of his many successes, he emerged from the conflict a war hero. During the war, he had to rely on militia from the various states. Many of these troops were unwilling to travel outside their state or local geographical area. At times, this was a disadvantage but the state militia fought heroically to defend their homeland. The fact they identified with the land they were defending often gave them an edge vis-à-vis the British. In 1775, the British were confident of victory. There was no American army to fight the British and no American government to direct the fighting. The British underestimated the determination of the colonists to win independence and they miscalculated the difficulties of suppressing a colonial rebellion. Despite the difficulties confronting Great Britain, it was a leading world power with greater resources compared to the colonies. The odds certainly seemed to favor the British. No nation was more powerful. A major advantage enjoyed by the colonists was the fact they too were English and had the support of a segment of the British population. George III wanted to retain control of the American colonies, but many people in Great Britain opposed waging a war against their countrymen living in the colonies. In many respects, the weaknesses of the colonial forces turned out to be advantages. The war ended with the signing of the Treaty of Paris in 1783. The colonists were victorious. The colonies were now free but faced an uncertain future. The new nation was blessed with many outstanding leaders who were determined to build a successful nation state. 490

WAR OF 1812

Great Britain and France were at war in 1812. The United States accused both countries of violating America's right as a neutral nation but many believed Great Britain committed more violations including the practice of impressments, placing restrictions on American trade, and supporting Indian tribes fighting the United States. Many Americans continued to distrust and dislike the British despite the signing of The Treaty of Paris 1783 and the Jay Treaty 1794. In June 1812, the United States declared war on Great Britain despite much opposition to that policy by segments of the American population. Opponents wanted the United States to remain neutral. The war had several causes. The British practice of impressment left many Americans angry because of their sense of humiliation. The British were supporting Indian tribes that wanted to create an Indian nation in West. The British blockaded the Atlantic Coast and impaired American trade with other nations. The war bitterly divided the American people. Support for the war came mainly from the southern and western sections of the country. Opposition was strong in the northeast. Some New England states entertained the idea of negotiating a separate peace with the British. At the time, sectional interests were strong. In 1814, Great Britain and France ended their conflict and there was no reason for the United States to continue the fight. In December, the United States and Great Britain signed the Treaty of Ghent ending the war. President Madison became very unpopular for initiating the war. Opponents referred to the conflict as Mr. Madison's War. Despite the unpopularity of the war, the Democratic Republican Party retained its popularity and won the 1816 presidential race. Although the Federalist Party opposed the unpopular war, the Federalists were beginning to fade from the political scene. Andrew Jackson, a war hero, emerged as a national figure and this helped him win the presidency in 1828. A major consequence of the war was a deterioration of Canadian-American relations. During the war, the United States attempted to invade Canada but was unsuccessful. A number of major military campaigns took place along the border. Some Americans were eager to win control over at least parts of Canada. There were a number of reasons for this including manifest destiny and Canadian-British support for Indian tribes fighting the United States. The result was a growing distrust between the two nations but there were no major issues that could not be peacefully resolved. 400

MEXICAN-AMERICAN WAR 1846

The Mexican-American War lasted from 1846 to 1848. A major cause of the conflict was the U.S. annexation of Texas in 1845. Texas had been a part of Mexico. The Mexican government objected to the annexation and in 1846 the two countries went to war. The United States, under the leadership of President Polk, was eager to expand America's territorial base. The war resulted in huge losses of territory for Mexico. The Rio Grande River became a boundary between the two countries. The United States won control of California, Utah, and Nevada. It also won control of parts of what are now Arizona, New Mexico, Wyoming, and Colorado. The United States won control of more than 500,000 square miles of territory excluding Texas. Many opponents of slavery opposed the war because of the slave issue. Proponents of slavery hoped the addition of more territory would help balance the growing power of the North. Slavery was already a divisive issue but the war exacerbated emotions on both sides. Mexico viewed the war as an act of aggression. Relations between Mexico and the United States remained tense long after the war. Zachary Taylor emerged as a war hero. In 1848, he ran for the presidency on the Whig ticket and succeeded in defeating Lewis Cass, the Democratic Party nominee. Slavery was a major issue during the campaign and divisions on the issue were evident. Taylor benefited by saying little about the issue that would eventually cause a civil war. 250

CIVIL WAR

The Civil War was the bloodiest war in American history. The immediate cause of the war was the decision of the southern states to secede from the Union after Lincoln's victory in the 1860 presidential election. He opposed slavery and was determined to end the slave system. The issue played a major role in the presidential election won by Lincoln. It was an important issue as far back as the 1789 Constitutional Convention. The southern states made it clear they could not support the proposed constitution unless it protected slavery. Back then, slaves made up about forty percent of the southern population. Slavery was an important part of the southern economy and had a major impact on the southern lifestyle. The southern states did not think they could survive economically without the slave system. The issue was so sensitive that some leaders did not want it debated publicly because debate would only inflame the issue for both sides. The problem of slavery became more acute as the United States moved westward. Supporters of the slave system saw the acquisition of western territory as strengthening their support of the system. Opponents wanted to prevent the extension of slavery to the western territories. When territories applied for statehood, the question of whether they would enter the Union as slave or free states became a controversial issue. The problem became more acute as a result of the Supreme Court's Dred Scott ruling in 1857. The ruling permitted the extension of slavery to the western territories. Those opposed to slavery were appalled at the prospect of slavery becoming legitimate in more areas. There was no longer a middle ground that could lead to compromise. It was obvious from a very early date that slavery and the ideas in the Declaration of Independence were incompatible. Slavery was connected to many other issues including states' rights, the southern lifestyle, and economics. Thomas Jefferson often expressed the fear that the slave issue could result in a civil war. Supporters and opponents of slavery reached a number of compromise agreements over the years but compromise often left both sides dissatisfied. The 1857 Dred Scott decision contributed to the outbreak of the civil war because states could now enter the Union as slave states. This would have shifted the sectional balance of power in favor of the southern states. The Supreme Court ruling plus the election of Lincoln in 1860 made the civil war inevitable. The war began in April 1961. President Lincoln issued two emancipation proclamations, one in September 1862 and the second in January 1863. The proclamations freed slaves in the southern states. The southern states surrendered in April 1865. A few days later John Booth assassinated President Lincoln. The southern states remained under the control of the national government until the end of the reconstruction era in 1877. Passage of the Thirteenth Amendment in 1865 officially ended slavery throughout the country. Despite the amendment, the southern states put into effect a number of laws to keep the races segregated. Segregation remained in place until the civil rights era and a number of Supreme Court rulings such as the 1954 Brown v. Board of Education. 515

SPANISH-AMERICAN WAR 1898

The Spanish-American War was brief, lasting from April to August 1998. Cuba was attempting to win independence from Spain but the Spanish government was determined to retain Cuba as a colony. Many Americans were sympathetic to Cuba's cause and the "yellow press" helped this. It exploited the crisis to advocate American intervention to help free Cuba. In February 1998, the USS Main, an American battleship, sunk while in a Cuban port. Many Americans accused Spain of being responsible although this was never proved. Two hundred sixty Americans died and the fatalities further inflamed public opinion against Spain. The United States declared war and then sent troops to occupy Cuba. When the war ended the United States won control over Cuba, Puerto Rico, Guam, and the Philippines. The acquisition of the Philippines projected American power into the Pacific region and this eventually caused tensions with Japan. It was also expanding its power in the region. Some Americans strongly opposed acquiring colonies because of historical anti-colonial sentiments dating back to the American Revolution. The U.S. Senate ratified the Treaty of Paris by a one vote margin. Opponents to the treaty included Mark Twain, Andrew Carnegie, former president Grover Cleveland, and John

Dewey. The end of the war did not end the fighting in the Philippines. Many natives wanted complete independence and they took up arms against the United States. The result was a brutal military conflict with numerous atrocities committed by both sides. The United States granted the Philippines independence in 1946. The Philippines, Guam, and Puerto Rico became American protectorates. Cuba was forces to accept the Platt Amendment granting the United States the right to have a military base on Guantanamo. The Spanish-American War launched the United States as an imperial power and a potential dominant force in world politics. 300

WORLD WAR I

World War I started in July 1914 after the assassination of Archduke Ferdinand of Austria while visiting Serbia. Many experts assumed the war would be brief. In short order, other nations joined the conflict including Great Britain, France, Germany, Belgium, Russia, and the Ottoman Empire. In the 1916 presidential campaign, President Wilson pledged to keep America neutral and out of the war. He won the election by a narrow margin largely because of this pledge. In January 1917, Germany announced its policy of unrestricted submarine warfare. Three months later, the United States entered the war. In January 1918, President Wilson went before a joint session of Congress and presented fourteen points he thought should be the basis for ending the war and building the peace. The war ended in November 1918. Germany surrendered on the basis of Wilson's Fourteen Points but the victorious powers at the Versailles peace conference largely ignored the fourteen points. The outcome of the war underlined the growing power of the United States but it also resulted in a good deal of cynicism on the part of the American people. The war did not make the world "safe for democracy" nor did it prove to be "the war to end all wars," two claims made by President Wilson.

In November 1919, the United States Senate rejected the Versailles Peace Treaty and refused to join the League of Nations. Americans once again embraced isolationism and this handicapped the United States in dealing with the rise of Fascism in Italy, Germany, and Japan in the 1930s. The appeal of Fascism was one of the consequences of the war. Another consequence was the 1917 Russian revolution. Provisions of the Versailles Treaty contributed to the outbreak of World War II. The League never accomplished what President Wilson hoped it would. President Wilson hoped the League would be a substitute for balance of power policies and military alliances. The question of whether the League would have been a more effective organization if the United States had joined will always remain unanswered. The peace treaty placed the entire blame for the war on Germany and imposed severe penalties the German people resented. In the 1930s, Adolf Hitler exploited the resentments, rebuilt the German economy, developed a powerful military machine, and launched World War II with the invasion of Poland in 1939. Great Britain and France were two of the victorious powers in World War I but the fact is that both nations never regained the power they had before the outbreak of the war. 425

WORLD WAR II

The 1919 Versailles Peace Treaty officially brought World War I to an end but left European politics in disarray. The treaty attempted to establish a new post war era but some nations were dissatisfied with the newly established status quo. The 1929 economic crash exacerbated the dissatisfaction. Fascism had great appeal throughout Europe. Hitler came to power in Germany in 1933 determined to rebuild Germany's military might and change the European status quo established after WW I. Italy and Japan, both victors in WW I, were also dissatisfied with the status quo. The three nations cooperated with each other and in 1940 signed a Tripartite Pact. In September 1939, Germany invaded Poland to begin World War II. Eventually all the major powers participated in the conflict. The United States entered the war in December 1941 after the Japanese attack on Pearl Harbor. Germany surrendered in May 1945. Japan surrendered three months later. The war had a profound impact on the United States. The United States and the Soviet Union, allies during the war, became the major cold war antagonists. The antagonism lasted throughout the cold war until the breakup of the Soviet Union in 1991. In 1945, the United States emerged as the most powerful nation in the world and assumed responsibility for protecting nations endangered or allegedly endangered by the Soviet Union and the communist bloc nations, including China. Foreign policy issues enhanced the power of the American president because the country looked to him for leadership. America's allies looked to the United States for aid and protection. One major result of World War II was the dismantling of Western colonial empires. Another major result was the decline of the former great powers such as Germany, Japan, France, and Great Britain. The decline began as a result of the costs of World War I. The end of WW II ushered in the nuclear era with all its dangerous potential. The two superpowers developed nuclear arsenals with enough power to destroy the world. This terrible destructive force influenced the foreign policies of both countries. Eventually, a number of other countries also developed nuclear arsenals. When World War II began, few political leaders could envision the major consequences of the war. The United States and the Soviet Union agreed to establish a United Nations to help maintain the peace but the superpowers generally ignored the organization when it was in their national interest to do so. Both countries adopted more traditional balance of power policies. 420

KOREAN WAR

The Korean War began in June 1950 when North Korea invaded South Korea to unify the country under communist rule. Before World War II, Japan controlled Korea but had to yield control after losing the war. The Soviet Union occupied Korea, north of the thirty eight parallel, until 1948. The United States occupied the southern half of the country but was planning to withdraw its troops when the Korean War began. In 1950, China and the Soviet Union encouraged and supported the decision of North Korea to try and unify the country. President Truman feared the Soviet Union might be encouraged to try to expand its power in Europe by using military force if the U.S. did not check the aggression in Asia. American officials had difficulty distinguishing between communist aggression and Korean nationalism. The leaders in North Korea and South Korea wanted a unified nation. The leaders in both parts of the country were nationalists supporting different ideologies. As a result of America's urging, the United Nations branded North Korea the aggressor and called for collective action to repel the invasion. The fact is it was the United States not the United Nations that dealt with the aggression. Even before the UN vote, President Truman dispatched military forces to halt the aggression. The war ended in July 1953 restoring the status quo that existed in 1950. Dwight Eisenhower won the 1952 presidential election in part because of his promise to bring the war to an end. The war soured Sino-American relations and made it difficult for the United States to establish diplomatic relations with the Chinese government. Sino-American relations remained antagonistic until President Nixon visited China in 1972. The United States and China did not establish formal diplomatic relations until 1979. Another result of the Korean conflict was the decision of the United States to strengthen its relations with Taiwan (Republic of China). In 1954, the two countries signed a defense treaty. The Korean War intensified Soviet-American hostilities and prompted the United States to strengthen the NATO military alliance. The war also proved to be a major cause of dispute between China and the Soviet Union although the United States was not aware of this at the time. One of the most important consequences of the war was the American decision to emphasize the importance of military power as part of the containment policy. As a part of that policy, President Eisenhower negotiated a number of military alliances extending America's protective military might. President Truman dispatched American military forces to fight in Korea without seeking a declaration of war from Congress. His policy served as an important precedent in future conflicts. 440

VIETNAM WAR

America's participation in the Vietnam War began gradually without any meaningful debate regarding the potential consequences of America's intervention until the United States was deeply involved in the conflict. President Eisenhower sent military advisors to Vietnam after the communists won control of North Vietnam in 1954. President Kennedy increased the American military commitment. President Johnson decided the United States, not the South Vietnamese government, would take primary responsibility for defending South Vietnam. To do this, he continually increased the American military commitment but this did not deter the North Vietnamese. Richard Nixon won the 1968 presidential election in part because of his promise to bring the war to an end. He decided to gradually withdraw American combat forces and to strengthen South Vietnam's military capabilities. The effort was a failure. In January 1973, the United States, and North Vietnam signed a cease-fire agreement ending America's involvement in the war. President Nixon hoped the agreement would permit an honorable American withdrawal. The American people no longer supported the war. In 1975, the North Vietnam government won control over all of Vietnam. The Vietnam War is another example of the ability of a president to wage war without receiving a declaration of war from Congress. As was the case in the Korean War, Vietnam once again demonstrated the unwillingness of the American people to support a prolonged war without the prospect of victory or a clear definition of what victory means. President Johnson's unpopularity was one reason he decided not to seek reelection in 1968. After the Vietnam debacle, American public opinion became much more isolationist. From the very beginning of the war, American officials underestimated the importance of nationalism as a motivating force for North Vietnam's leaders. They viewed the American intervention in Indochina as another form of Western colonialism. The Vietnam War was one of the most divisive wars in American history. The Vietnam War and the 2003 Iraq War have one thing in common. When the United States intervened in Vietnam, government policy makers failed to consult with experts familiar with Asian politics and history. When the United States intervened in Iraq, many officials responsible for the war knew little about the Middle East and even less about Sunni-Shia differences. 370

U.S. INVADES GRENADA 1983

In October, 1983, President Reagan, responding to a request from the Governor General of Grenada, dispatched American military forces to overthrow a communist government that had seized power. The American troops quickly won control of the country, captured Cuban military forces in Grenada, and established sufficient stability for the people to conduct democratic elections for a new government in 1984. After the election, the United States withdrew all its forces. President Reagan wanted to send a message to the Soviet Union. The United States would use military force in response to communist governments that came to power through the use of violence and with the support of the Soviet Union. The message was important because the U.S., ever since the Vietnam conflict, was reluctant to use its military might. The overthrow of the communist government in Grenada was an example of the Reagan Doctrine and the president's willingness to commit American forces to block the spread of communism, using force if necessary. Many governments criticized the American decision but the people in Grenada welcomed the restoration of their democratic political system and the complete withdrawal of American military forces. Grenada was again free and democratic. 200

U.S. INVADES PANAMA 1989

In May 1989, Panama held national elections. General Noriega, the real power in Panama, supported Carlos Duque. Impartial observers, including an American delegation led by former President Carter agreed that Guillermo Endara won the election but General Noriega insisted that Duque was the victor. The international community demanded that Noriega yield power but he refused. In December, Panama declared it was at war with the United States. Five days later American forces invaded Panama, captured Noriega, and put him on trial in the United States for drug smuggling. A jury found him guilty and he received a forty year jail sentence. Guillerma Endara became president. The invasion of Panama met with much international criticism. The Soviet Union, despite improved relations with the United States, criticized the invasion as did the Organization of American States, and the United Nations General Assembly. Critics accused President H.W. Bush of acting because the Soviet Union was no longer a check on American power. If the Soviet Union invaded a country to remove a government from power, American officials would have been quick to condemn the action. Soviet officials accused the United States of having a double standard. Some international agencies were critical of the United States because of the high number of non-military Panamanian casualties. The various estimates were much higher than the figures put out by American officials. The outcome of the war resulted in a surge in President H.W. Bush's popularity at home but he nevertheless was defeated in the 1992 presidential election. 255

GULF WAR 1991

In August 1990, Iraq military forces invaded Kuwait and annexed it. Saddam Hussein justified the invasion by claiming that Kuwait was historically a part of Iraq. He also accused of Kuwait of illegally extracting oil from Iraqi territory. The claim did not have much legitimacy. What was true was that Iraq had massive debts to pay as a result of the decade long Iraq-Iranian war. Iraq easily and quickly defeated the Kuwait military resistance. Iraq's invasion of Kuwait created an immediate threat to Saudi Arabia. If Iraq invaded and defeated Saudi Arabia it would control about half the world's supply of oil. The United States with the backing of the United Nations and the Soviet Union insisted that Iraq withdraw its troops from Kuwait but Saddam Hussein rejected the demand. He demonstrated his contempt for the international community by annexing Kuwait. In response, the United States dispatched 250,000 troops to protect Saudi Arabia. In February 1991, an American led coalition invaded Iraq to force the government to withdraw from Kuwait. The coalition numbered about 700,000 troops, including 500,000 American forces. The invasion was successful. The troops liberated Kuwait and thoroughly defeated the Iraqi forces. The fighting lasted for about one hundred hours. Iraq withdrew its forces but Saddam Hussein remained in power, defied the United Nations and the inspection system it put into place. He also launched a chemical attack on the Kurds in northern Iraq because of their opposition to his rule. The attacks resulted in the death of thousands of Kurds. The international community did nothing in response to the chemical attacks. One important aspect of the conflict was the cooperation between the United States and the

Soviet Union. During the cold war, Iraq and the Soviet Union were allies. The cooperation between the two superpowers was another sign the cold war was over. Despite the success of the coalition, some critics were dissatisfied because Saddam Hussein remained in power but removing him from power was not part of the UN mandate nor was it a goal of American policy. Despite Iraq's defeat, Hussein continued to defy the United Nations and evade sanctions imposed on Iraq after the war. He assumed he could go on defying the demands of the United States and the international community but he over estimated his power and authority. In 2003, the United States invaded Iraq and removed Hussein from power. A new Iraqi government sentenced him to death. He was executed in 2006. 410

AFGHAN WAR 2001

On October 2001, a coalition of nations led by the United States, invaded Afghanistan to overthrow the Taliban government and capture or kill Osama bin Laden, the leader of al-Qaeda. Americans held him responsible for the 9/11 attacks on the United States. The invasion succeeded in overthrowing the government but bin Laden escaped. In 2003, the United States invaded Iraq and as a result, the war in Afghanistan diminished in importance. As the Afghan War lost it high priority, the Taliban reemerged as a threat. After the 08 election, President Obama agreed to a further increase in the U.S. military commitment to Afghanistan despite the fact he opposed the American military mission in Iraq while a member of the Senate. He agreed to increase the American military presence in Afghanistan because a Taliban led government in Kabul could threaten Pakistan and might plan further attacks on the United States. This was a crucial factor because Pakistan is a nuclear power. Critics of Obama charged this his policies were no different from those of President George W. Bush. They feared the United States would get bogged down in a prolonged war in Afghanistan that could not be won. President Obama pledged to begin troop withdrawal by 2011, but he did not specify how he would manage the withdrawal. He could implement the withdrawal schedule in different ways. Some critics claimed that defeating the Taliban required a commitment to nation building that could take fifteen to thirty years. Although President H. Bush initiated the war, after Barak Obama's election in 2008, Afghanistan became his war. By 2010, a greater number of critics were suggesting that the United States could not win the war. The cost of trying to win the war continued to increase both financially and in the number of people killed and wounded. 300

IRAQ WAR 2003

After the 9/11 attack terrorist attack on the United States, if not before, American officials decided to militarily invade Iraq and remove Saddam Hussein from power. In March 2003, British and American troops invaded Iraq. A number of nations assisted the American and British forces but their contribution was at best marginal. The primary justification for the invasion was the claim that Iraq was aiding terrorist groups and building a WMD arsenal. The first claim was at best dubious because of the lack of supporting evidence; the second proved to be untrue despite the fact many nations believed it was accurate. The invasion was successful; Saddam Hussein was overthrown, captured, and executed. The war began without the approval of the United Nations. Several close allies of the United States and many nations around the world opposed the invasion and the subsequent occupation. Many experts have been critical of the decision-making process that led to the war. Anyone opposed to the invasion, such as Secretary of State Powell, were kept out of the decision making loop. There never was a meeting of all the important decision makers to debate the wisdom of going to war. President Bush was determined to have a war. Very few observers, if any, anticipated an occupation that would last as long as it did. This added to the condemnation of the United States. Governments and public opinion around the world viewed the American military as an occupation rather than a liberating force. Many Americans shared this sentiment. The war became increasingly unpopular in the United States and weakened the Bush presidency. It began without the authorization or approval of the United Nations and drove a wedge between the United States and some major European powers. Many experts agree that policy makers relied on a flawed process in their planning for the war. After defeating Iraq's military forces, the United States then assumed responsibility for governing the country. That proved to be a much greater challenge than winning the military battles. America's prestige, as measured by various public opinion polls, declined precipitously around the world. In 2006, Democrats won control of Congress. Two years later, they won control of the White House. Before leaving office, the George W. Bush administration succeeded in negotiating an agreement with the Iraqi government for the withdrawal of American combat forces and a significant reduction in American military personnel but the Iraqi government failed to sign the agreement while Bush was in office. President Obama signed an agreement for withdrawal of all U. S. troops by end of 2011.

FOREIGN POLICY DOCTRINES

There is no way of knowing why a foreign policy becomes a "doctrine." A foreign policy morphs into a doctrine when enough people label it as such and it remains viable for a long period. Many presidents and policy makers have attempted to legitimatize a policy by simply linking it to a doctrine. Some foreign policy doctrines are associated with particular events but historians may identify others with a historical period such as the cold war. If a doctrine outlives a particular historical event or a historic period, it may endure because its basic values remain relevant. Presidents like to have a foreign policy identified with their name because they believe it contributes to their prestige. Whether intended or not, some foreign policy doctrines may add to the president's power and prestige. This was particularly true of the Monroe Doctrine and the Truman Doctrine. Doctrines may be in the form of a presidential statement, a congressional resolution, a speech or some combination of those elements. American presidents did not always invoke the Monroe Doctrine when intervening in Latin America but others might be quick to make the linkage. The doctrine contains a set of principles that remained applicable long after Monroe formulated the doctrine. The cold war rivalry between the United States and the Soviet Union revitalized the Monroe Doctrine particularly after Castro came to power in 1959. Many cold war doctrines became irrelevant when the cold war ended but some principles contained in the doctrines will always be relevant in the making of foreign policy.

MONROE DOCTRINE

The Monroe Doctrine is perhaps the best known foreign policy doctrine in American history because of its relevance over a long period. In 1823, President Monroe laid out the basic principles of the doctrine. The United States wanted to prevent European powers from colonizing countries in the Americas. At the time, European interest in establishing colonies arose because Spain could no longer control its colonies in the Western Hemisphere and many became independent. American and British officials feared that European powers would try to win control over these countries and thereby threaten the United States and upset the balance of power in Europe. President Monroe was in effect declaring that Latin America was an American sphere of influence although officials did not like to use that term because of its association with balance of power policies. In return for keeping the Europeans out of the Western Hemisphere, the United States promised not to interfere in European affairs. The irony of the Monroe Doctrine is the fact the U.S. did not have the military power to enforce it but Great Britain did and was willing to do so because of its own national interests. American and British goals were similar. At the time, Great Britain was a major trading partner of many Latin American nations. In 1902, President Roosevelt developed a corollary to the Monroe Doctrine that justified American intervention in Latin American countries to maintain order. This meant the US could intervene when a Latin American government instituted policies that displeased the United States. Latin American nations opposed the Monroe Doctrine and the Roosevelt Corollary. Over the years, American officials often relied on the doctrine to justify intervening with military force when American interests were allegedly threatened.

TRUMAN DOCTRINE

President Truman appeared before a joint session of Congress in March 1947 to announce what policy makers labeled the Truman Doctrine. Some historians use the doctrine as a date for the beginning of the cold war but there is no consensus on just when the cold war began. Differences between the United States and the Soviet Union were evident long before World War II ended. Truman's doctrine consists of two parts. One part was a specific pledge to aid Greece and Turkey. A civil war was raging in Greece between the government and a communist insurgency. There was no insurgency in Turkey but the Soviet Union was making territorial demands opposed by the Turkish government. The Soviets were demanding to play a role in defense of the Bosporus and the Dardanelles Straits. During and after World War II, Turkey and the Soviet Union were often at odds. The second part of the Truman Doctrine was America's willingness to provide aid to any country threatened by communism. This gave the doctrine a universal sweep. George Kennan, the architect of containment, opposed the Truman Doctrine. He thought it was too open-ended and overextended America's resources and commitments. He also opposed some military policies associated with the doctrine. He opposed the Vietnam War because he did not think Vietnam was a vital American national interest. The Soviet Union was quick to denounce the doctrine when it was formulated. Soviet leaders promised to use whatever means were necessary to oppose it. The outbreak of the Korean War in 1950 resulted in the militarization of the doctrine and its extension beyond Europe into Asia. Policymakers often invoked the principles of the Truman Doctrine whenever the U.S. was confronted with national security challenges including military actions across the globe. The Truman Doctrine was an important part of America's containment policy along with the 1948 Marshall Plan and the establishment of NATO in 1949. Policy makers invoked the Truman Doctrine to legitimatize policies to deal with communist threats.

EISENHOWER DOCTRINE

In 1956, Israel, France, and Great Britain invaded Egypt after President Nasser nationalized the Suez Canal. One purpose of the invasion was to overthrow President Nasser but the effort failed and the failure had a profound impact on the Middle East. It enhanced Nasser's prestige and Egypt's power and influence in the region. The Soviet Union supported Egypt's nationalization of the Suez Canal and as a result Soviet prestige in the region soared. France and Great Britain were no longer major players in the region. The turn of events worried American officials. President Eisenhower thought the United States should fill the resulting vacuum of power. In response to the crisis, President Eisenhower appeared before a joint session of Congress in January 1957 to outline what policy makers began to refer to as the Eisenhower Doctrine. Great Britain and France, because of the failed invasion and their reduced power, could no longer be expected to play a significant role in the region. The president offered to protect Middle Eastern countries friendly to the United States and endangered by governments supporting the Soviet Union, including Egypt. Chairman Khrushchev, the leader of the Soviet Union, wanted to reduce or eliminate American influence in that part of the world and he had Egypt's support. The Eisenhower Doctrine seemed to be important because Great Britain and France had lost much of their power and influence in the Middle East because of past colonial policies and the consequences of World War II. Leaders in both countries underestimated Nasser's popularity and influence throughout the region and in many third world countries. He was a nationalist and eagerly accepted whatever support the Soviet Union could offer. Khrushchev believed that by supporting Egypt, the Soviet Union would become a major actor in region and thereby reduce American influence. President Nasser exploited the superpower rivalry in support of Egypt's national interests. Soviet-American rivalry in the

Middle East was another example of the bipolar distribution of power that existed at the time. The Eisenhower Doctrine had little impact on the region. Nasser was anti-American but he was no friend of the Soviet Union. He willingly accepted Soviet economic and military aid but also curbed Soviet influence in the region. He saw no contradiction between the two. In 1958, President Eisenhower did dispatch troops to Lebanon at the request of the Lebanese government but the problems there were primarily local in nature and had little to do with the cold war. Eisenhower's doctrine had little impact in the Middle East.

JOHNSON DOCTRINE

In an address to the American people in May 1965, President Johnson announced that the United States would not tolerate the establishment of another communist government in the Western Hemisphere. A civil war was raging in the Dominican Republic that involved several factions including communists and anti-communists. President Johnson dispatched 20,000 American troops to the Dominican Republic to put his doctrine into effect and to establish order. The intervention violated the principles associated with President Roosevelt's Good Neighbor policy but American officials feared that without the American military intervention, the communists and their supporters would win power. In June 1966, elections in the Dominican Republican resulted in a victory for the anti-communist forces, supported by the C.I.A. Although the United States intervened in Latin America several times after the Dominican intervention, no president relied on the Johnson Doctrine to justify military intervention to deal with communist threats.

NIXON DOCTRINE

Throughout the 1960s, a growing number of Americans opposed U.S. policies in the Vietnam War. The Nixon Doctrine, sometimes called the Guam Doctrine, was developed in response to that opposition. The costs of the war plus the fact there was no clear definition of what would constitute a victory, increased opposition to the war effort. The United States lacked an exit strategy. Opposing President Johnson's Vietnam policies was a major factor in Nixon's victory in the 1968 presidential election. During the presidential campaign, Nixon claimed to have a plan for ending the war that was associated with the Johnson Administration and Vice President Humphrey, Nixon's opponent in the 1968 election. In an address to the American people in November 1969, President Nixon articulated the three basic principles of his doctrine. The United States would honor its military and economic commitments to the nations of Asia. Second, he promised to continue to protect America's allies in Asia by providing them with a nuclear shield so they would not develop independent nuclear arsenals. Third, the Asian nations would in the future have to provide the manpower to fight local wars. The United States would not again make the military commitment it made in Vietnam. President Johnson made the United States responsible for defending South Vietnam rather than relying on the government in Saigon. The Nixon Doctrine placed greater responsibility on South Vietnam for its own security. That decision enabled the United States to withdraw its forces from Vietnam, a policy supported by the American people. The Nixon Doctrine as it pertained to Vietnam became obsolete when North Vietnam succeeded in unifying the country in 1975. Some critics claim the only purpose of the doctrine was to legitimatize the exit of U.S. military forces from an unpopular war. The doctrine, however, was relevant to problems other than Vietnam. For example, it was relevant to Iran and the Persian Gulf. The United States relied on Iran to help maintain peace and stability in the Persian Gulf. One result of this was a massive increase in arms sales from the United States to Iran. U.S.-Iranian relations were close and this contributed to the anti-American backlash after the overthrow of the Iranian government in 1979. The Nixon Doctrine had links to President Eisenhower's New Look policy that he instituted after the Korean War. Some policy makers linked the Eisenhower Doctrine to the policy of détente that President Nixon helped put into place with his visits to Moscow and Beijing in 1972.

CARTER DOCTRINE

The Carter Doctrine consists of a series of policies and statements made in response to the Soviet invasion of Afghanistan in January 1979. President Carter first enunciated the doctrine in his 1980 State of the Union address to Congress. He created a Rapid Deployment Force to protect American interests in the Persian Gulf. He increased American defense spending, ordered a boycott of the Moscow Olympics, imposed a grain embargo on the Soviet Union, and withdrew the SALT II treaty from the Senate where it was considering ratification. The most important aspect of the Carter Doctrine was the decision to aid the Mujahedeen fighting the Soviet military forces in Afghanistan. In addition to financial aid, American experts trained and equipped the Mujahedeen to better enable them to deal with the Soviet threat. President Reagan dramatically escalated aid to the Mujahedeen when he agreed to supply them with Stinger missiles that were effective in downing Soviet aircraft transporting Soviet troops. The Stinger missiles increased Soviet casualties and were a major factor in Gorbachev's decision to withdraw Soviet military forces and end the intervention. The withdrawal was one of the factors that led to the disintegration of the Soviet Union in 1991. The Soviet invasion of Afghanistan combined with the Carter Doctrine increased Soviet-American tensions and hostility. The doctrine represented a significant change in Carter's approach to dealing with the Soviet Union. He previously chided the American people for their "inordinate fear of communism." By 1980, despite the Carter Doctrine, the president lost the confidence of the American people. Ronald Reagan easily defeated Carter in the presidential election that year. After his election, President Reagan substantially increased America's military spending but in fact the spending increase began the last year of the Carter administration.

REAGAN DOCTRINE

There is no specific date for the Reagan Doctrine nor does it have specific policies associated with it. Basically, President Reagan promised to assist those forces seeking to overthrow communist governments that came to power as a result of Soviet aid, including military and covert assistance. The doctrine rejected President Nixon's policy of détente based on an acceptance of the status quo including Soviet domination of Eastern Europe. The doctrine was also a belated response to the 1968 Brezhnev Doctrine that promised to keep in power any communist government supported by the Soviet Union. Examples of the Reagan Doctrine include aid the United States gave to groups in Angola, Nicaragua, Ethiopia, and other countries fighting communist forces. President Reagan's support for democratic reforms in Poland was a part of that doctrine. The Reagan Doctrine also deviated from the policy of containment that began with the Truman Doctrine in 1947. The containment policy accepted the fact that the Soviet Union was going to retain control over its communist empire. Acceptance of the status quo was an American foreign policy goal from President Truman to President Nixon. During the 1952 presidential campaign, some Republicans advocated "rolling back communism" but that proved to be nothing more than a campaign slogan intended to win votes. After his electoral victory, President Eisenhower accepted the status quo and tried to strengthen it by meeting with Premier Khrushchev, the Soviet leader, in Geneva in

1955. By that time both superpowers had nuclear arsenals. The Reagan Doctrine supported groups fighting communism but, with one exception, did not involve American military forces other than those engaged in covert activities. Critics of the Reagan Doctrine feared it would intensify cold war conflicts and reduce cooperation between the superpowers. His critic failed to mention that the Soviet Union, despite the policy of détente, never ceased supporting communist movements around the world regardless of how that support impacted Soviet-American relations. Critics were asking President Reagan to do what they did not demand of the Soviet Union. Soviet leaders believed they had an obligation to help spread communism regardless of the costs or American opposition. The Reagan Doctrine put an additional strain on the Soviet Union at a time when its economy was in free-fall. President Reagan never gave a speech specifically formulating what came to be known as the Reagan Doctrine but his 1985 State of the Union address outlined policies that came to be associated with it. The label was first used by the columnist Charles Krauthammer after Reagan' State of the Union address. Most leaders of the Democratic Party rejected the Reagan Doctrine and the policies associated with it. For example, they opposed Reagan's decision to send troops into Grenada. In 1983, a communist coup overthrew a democratically elected government. The United States invaded Grenada and restored its democratic government. Although the invasion took place in 1983, it is associated with the Reagan Doctrine. The Reagan Doctrine was used to justify aiding some groups simply because they opposed communism. President Reagan summed up his goal in relation to the Soviet Union when he said "we win and they lose."

BUSH DOCTRINE

The Bush (43) Doctrine, formulated after 9/11, and articulated by President George W. Bush at various times including his address to West Point in 2002. It is probably the most controversial of all the American foreign policy doctrines. Initially, the doctrine was a justification for the U.S. invasion of Afghanistan in 2001. The doctrine became increasingly controversial after the U.S. invaded Iraq in 2003. The doctrine has four major points: justification for preemptive wars, promotion of democracy, regime change, and American primacy. Some would add a fifth point: a willingness to pursue a unilateralist foreign policy. Although controversial, the Bush Doctrine contained elements long associated with American foreign policy. In fact, these elements are often characteristic of great power politics. The controversies associated with the Bush Doctrine resulted from his interpretation of its principles rather than the principles themselves. One of the most controversial principles was that of preemption. The right to launch a militarily attack on those about to attack you has a long legitimate history based on a nation's right to protect its national security. The problem with preemption is that it requires accurate intelligence on the imminence of an attack. There was absolutely no evidence Iraq was about to attack the United States or any other country in 2003. In addition, there was no evidence Iraq was attempting to build nuclear weapons although many governments believed otherwise. Critics charge President Bush ordered the militarily attack to remove Saddam Hussein from power and sought any excuse to do so. Most policy analysts believe invading a country to oust a government is illegitimate. There are other ways to achieve that objective such as supporting and encouraging a coup d'état. President Bush's policy could more accurately be labeled "prevention" rather than "preemption." The two policies are dissimilar. Unilateralism is not necessarily illegitimate but critics are more likely to consider policies legitimate if supported by other nations, particularly close allies. Not only did President Bush not have much international support for invading Iraq, close allies of the U.S. opposed the invasion because they did not see Iraq as an immediate threat to any other nation, including neighbors. Some critics of President Bush claim he was eager to invade Iraq even before 9/11. Individuals in the intelligence community kept insisting there was no evidence of any connection between Saddam Hussein and 9/11 but some members of the Bush administration kept insisting that the search should go on to find a connection. Although Saddam Hussein was captured by the American military and executed by the Iraqi government, that did not end the American military intervention. American troops remained in Iraq for ten years but failed to halt the sectarian violence. Critics of American policy claim one of the major consequences of the military intervention was an increase in Iran's influence in Iraq. The American intervention in Iraq brought Shia groups to power that were sympathetic to Iran. Saddam Hussein was a Sunni and ruthlessly suppressed the Shia, the majority religious group in Iraq. Iran is a Shia country and a rival to Saudi Arabia, the leader of the Sunni. When American combat forces withdrew from Iraq in 2011, political unrest and sectarian violence remained a problem.

DATES TO KNOW

1774 CONTINENTAL CONGRESS CONVENED

1775 SECOND CONTINENTAL CONGRESS CONVENED

1776 DECLARATION OF INDEPENDENCE

1777 CONTINENTAL CONGRESS APPROVED ARTICLES OF CONFEDERATION

1781 STATES APPROVED THE ARTICLES OF CONFEDERATION

1783 TREATY OF PARIS

1786 SHAYS REBELLION

1786 ANNAPOLISH CONVENTION

1787 CONSTITUTIONAL CONVENTION CONVENED

1788 NEW HAMPSIRE, THE NINTH STATE, APPROVED THE CONSTITUTION

1788 NEW YORK AND VIRGINIA RATIFIED THE CONSTITUTION AFTER THE NEW HAMPSHIRE RATIFICATION

1789 THE CONSTITUTION BECAME OPERATIVE

1789 CONGRESS APPROVED THE BILL OF RIGHTS

1789 NORTH CAROLINA RATFIED THE CONSTITUTION

1789 CONGRESS CONVENES WITH SIXTY-FIVE MEMBERS

1789 CONGRESS APPROVES THE JUDICIARY ACT

1790 RHODE ISLAND WAS THE LAST STATE TO RATIFY THE CONSTITUTION

1791 STATES COMPLETED RATIFICATION OF THE BILL OF RIGHTS

1792 FEDERALIST PARTY WAS ORGANIZED

1794 THE UNITED STATES AND GREAT BRITAIN SIGNED THE JAY TREATY

1800s

1858 DRED SCOTT DECISION

1869 SINCE 1869 THE SUPREME COURT HAS HAD NINE JUDGES

1900s

1911 THE HOUSE OF RERESENTATIVES INCREASED ITS MEMBERSHIP TO 435

1913 W. WILSON ELECTED PRESSIDENT

1913 MEMBERSHIP IN HOUSE OF REPRESENTAIVES INCREASED TO 435

1917 U.S. ENTERS WW I

1918 PRESIDENT WILSON ANNOUNCES HIS FOURTEEN POINTS FOR PEACE

1919 U.S. SENATE REJECTS VERSAILLES TREATY

1929 STOCK MARKET CRASH

1929 STATES APPROVE NINETEENTH AMENDMENT GIVING WOMEN THE RIGHT TO VOTE

1932 F.D.R. ELECTED PRESIDENT

1940 F.D.R. ELECTED PRESIDENT FOR THIRD TERM

1941 U.S. ENTERS WWII

1944 F.D.R. ELECTED FOR FOURTH TERM

1945 F.D.R. DIES

1945 WW II ENDS

1948 HARRY TRUMAN WINS PRESIDENTIAL ELECTION

1950s

1950 KOREAN WAR BEGINS

1952 EISENHOWER WINS PRESIDENTIAL ELECTION

1953 KOREAN WAR ENDS

1954 BROWN V. BOARD OF EDUCATION OUTLAWS SCHOOL SEGREGATION

1956 EISENHOWER REELECTED PRESIDENT

1956 SUEZ CRISIS

1957 EISENHOWER DOCTRINE

1959 HAWAII AND ALASKA ADMITTED AS STATES

1959 CASTRO COMES TO POWERIN CUBA

1960s

1960 JOHN F. KENNEDY FIRST CATHOLIC TO BE ELECTED PRESIDENT

1962 CUBAN MISSILE CRISIS

1963 MARTIN KING LEADS CIVIL RIGHTS MARCH WASHINGTON

1964 SENATE APPROVES GULF OF TONKIN RESOLUTION

1968 MARTIN LUTHER KING ASSASSANATED

1968 ROBERT KENNEDY ASSASSANATED\

1968 NIXON ELECTED PRESIDENT

1970s

1971 SENATE APPROVES TWENTY-SIXTH AMENDMENT LOWERING VOTING AGE TO EIGHTEEN

1972 NIXON'S HISTORIC VISIT TO CHINA

1972 NIXON REELECTED PRESIDENT

1973 VICE PRESIDENT AGNEW RESIGNS

1974 PRESIDENT NIXON RESIGNS

1976 JIMMY CARTER ELECTED PRESIDENT

1979 IRAN HOSTAGE CRISIS BEGINS

1980s

1980 RONALD REAGAN ELECTED PRESIDENT

1980 U.S. HOSTAGES IN IRAN FREED

1981 PRESIDENT REAGAN WOUNDED BY GUNMAN

1983 UNITED STATES INVADES GRENADA

1984 RONALD REAGAN REELECTED

1988 GEORGE H.W. BUSH ELECTED PRESIDENT

1988 IRAQ LAUNCHES CHEMICAL ATTACK ON KURDS

1990s

1990 IRAQ INVADES KUWAIT

1991 U.S. MILITARY LIBERATES KUWAIT

1992 WILLIAM CLINTON WINS PRSIDENTIAL ELECTION

1996 CLINTON REELECTED

1999 U.S. BEGINS BOMBING OF YUGOSLAVIA

2000s

2000 GEORGE W. BUSH ELECTED PRESIDENT

2001 AL QAEDA LAUNCHES 9/11 ATTACK

2001 U.S. INVADES AFGHANISTAN

2003 U.S. INVADES IRAQ

2003 SADDAM HUSSEIN CAPTURED

2004 GEORGE W. BUSH WINS REELECTION

2006 SADDAM HUSSEIN EXECUTED

2008 BARAK OBAMA ELECTED PRESIDENT

2008 U.S. TO WITHDRAW TROOPS FROM IRAQ 2011 63,250

Lightning Source UK Ltd.
Milton Keynes UK
UKOW05f1957241113

221733UK00001B/112/P